AF553703

Globalisation and Economic Growth

GLOBALISATION AND ECONOMIC GROWTH

By

Dr. M. Lakshmi Narasaiah

M.A., Ph.D.,
Professor and Head
Department of Economics
Sri Krishnadevaraya University
Post-graduate Centre,
Kurnool— 518 002
A.P. (India)

DISCOVERY PUBLISHING HOUSE
NEW DELHI-110002

First Published-2003

Reprinted-2011

ISBN 81-7141-673-X

Published by

DISCOVERY PUBLISHING HOUSE
4831/24, Ansari Road, Prahlad Street,
Darya Ganj, New Delhi-110002 (India)
Phone: 3279245 • Fax: 91-11-3253475
E-mail:dphtemp@indiatimes.com

Printed at:
Mehra Offset Press
Delhi

PREFACE

Globalisation has become today's buzzword. It has also become a battle ground for two radically opposed groups. There are the anti-globalists, who fear globalisation and stress only its downside, seeking therefore powerful interventions aimed at taming, if not (unwittingly) crippling it. Then there are the "globalists" (a class to which I belong) who celebrate globalisation instead, emphasize its upside, while seeking only to ensure that its few rough edges be handled through appropriate policies that serve to make globalisation yet more attractive.

Many anti-globalists consider the central problem of globalisation to be its amorality, or even its immorality. But these critics have to blanket an approach to globalisation. The word covers a variety of phenomena that characterize an integrating world economy: trade, short-term capital flows, direct foreign investment, immigration, cultural convergence *et al.* The sins of one of the above cannot be visited upon the virtues of another. Some are benign even when largely unregulated whereas others can be fatal if left wholly to the marketplace.

In particular, the freeing of trade is largely benign: if I exchange some of my toothpaste for some of your toothbrushes, we will both be better off than if we did not trade at all. It would require a wild imagination, and a deranged mind, to think that such freeing of trade leads to debilitating economic crises. Equally, it is illogical to believe, as non-economists who fear globalisation do , that freeing of trade is bad because the freeing of short-term capital flows led to a debilitating financial and economic crises and could do so again. In fact, while there are some obvious simulates between free trade and free capital flows e.g. that segmentation of markets creates efficiency losses—the economic and political dissimilarities are even more compelling and policymakers cannot ignore them.

Anti-globalist critics are in fact often reacting viscerally to a much larger issue: the victory of capitalism over its arch rival, communism. For campus idealists who have always looked for alternatives to what they conventionally consider to be the greed and lack of social conscience that characterize capitalism, the situation is psychologically intolerable. Some have turned to street theatre, nihilism and the anti-intellectualism that has been manifest in the last few years. The more sophisticated have succumbed to a stereotypical representation of corporation as the evil forces of capitalism that have captured the state, democratic institutions, and even international bodies such as the World Trade Organization.

What these critics often forget is that certain economic freedoms are basic to prosperity and social well-being under any conditions, and are thus of the highest moral value. Property rights and markets, for instance, provide incentives to produce and allocate resources efficiently, and can in turn strengthen democracy by allowing a means of sustenance out side pervasive government structures. The quality and breadth of democracy can then be enlarged as excluded groups, such as women and the poor, are pulled into literacy, gainful employment and better health through higher public spending or the spread of economic incentives.

Critics nevertheless go on to maintain that the global spread of free markets and free trade is responsible for continuing poverty in poor countries, and for alleged growth in inequality between and within countries. Labour unions in the rich countries also fear that trade in cheap labour-using goods from poor countries.

Dr. M. Lakshmi Narasaiah

CONTENTS

THE CHALLENGES OF GLOBALISATION

Globalisation gives rise in some quarters to fears that can lead to suspicion, protectionism, and policies that are ultimately self-destructive. Such fears cannot be allowed to frustrate the great potential of a world in which countries drawing closer together. We believe that countries can face the challenges of globalisation positively, demanding as those challenges may be.

All countries can benefit from full participation in the world's markets, including its financial markets. Protectionist pressures must be resisted and reversed, and the principles of openness and multilateralism promoted by the World Trade Organisation, the IMF, and the World Bank must be honoured. And financial market integration should be seen as a positive force: it offers access to global financial intermediation and a stimulus for more competitive and efficient domestic financial sectors, and it promotes efficiency and growth worldwide.

How encouraging it is, therefore, to see that so many developing countries in transition have been freeing up their trade and exchange systems within the framework of our structural adjustment programmes.

No country can afford to forgo the benefits of integration into global market: the alternative is marginalisation and stagnation. But all countries must take the steps to minimise the associated risks. More than ever before, countries need tightly disciplined macro economic policies to maintain a stable environment for investors, whether domestic or foreign. And while foreign capital can be a useful—and sometimes vital complement to domestic saving, it is not a substitute for it: domestic saving remains the key to investment and sustainable growth. It is also clear that strong financial institutions are essential to avoid market disturbances at home and to secure an effective defence against external pressures. Competitive banking and financial systems that are sound, well regulated, and properly supervised are indispensable for countries to be able to expose their economies safely to the pressures that can arise in global markets.

The challenges to globalisation therefore add to the need for the developing and transition countries to press ahead with their adjustment and reform efforts. For many, this means creating conditions to attract foreign financing and use it effectively. But a growing number of countries, have been facing a different problem: how to cope with large-scale capital inflows. Such inflows, especially when they are easily reversible, provide no grounds for relaxation of adjustment and reform.

They should not be used to finance domestic consumption. In many cases, they call for stronger fiscal discipline; and in some cases, exchange rates should be allowed to take part of the strain. Many developing countries and countries in transition also, of course, need to do more to deepen and widen the role of market forces and to foster more competitive market environments, in order to promote transparent and efficient mechanisms for resource allocation.

Is globalisation any less demanding for the industrial countries? Not at all! It adds to the urgency of the task of taking full advantage of the current expansion to tackle the deep-rooted problems that are limiting the pace, the quality, and perhaps, the sustainability of their growth.

All has to applaud the increased efforts and commitments to reduce fiscal deficits, but in most cases underlying imbalances remain large and the pace of consolidation too slow. More must be done not only to redress present imbalances but also to meet the growing demands of the future.

Another deep-rooted problem—structural unemployment—must also be tackled sooner, rather than later. Budget laxity and high unemployment tend to feed on each other. While cyclical conditions provide the opportunity, governments must not flinch from the task of improving the functioning of labour markets. How? It is not an easy task: by reforming regulations and policies that impede employment creation and job search.

Monetary stability, macro-economic discipline, sound financial systems, and efficiently working market mechanisms are essential for all countries that embrace globalisation. But they are not sufficient for any. To fight the fears that globalisation sometimes inspires, countries need policies that promote not just economic efficiency, financial stability, and growth but also equity and high-quality growth. In too many countries, the quality of growth suffers from widening distributional inequalities related partly to high unemployment but also stagnating wages of unskilled workers. And too many countries continue to suffer from poor governance, corruption and increasing crime.

Of course, economic policy can provide only part of what is needed to rid the world of these blights. But it is a vital part. To promote equity, efficiency, and sustainable growth, governments carry an inescapable responsibility for investment in human capital—through education, health care, and well-targeted social safety nets—and also for establishing and maintaining honest and effective systems of public administration, law, order and justice. If these essential services are to be affordable, there is certainly no room for unproductive expenditures—military or otherwise—and wasteful subsidies: they must bear the brunt of fiscal consolidation. So globalisation demands a lot from governments if it is to deliver its promise of stronger and high-quality growth.

GLOBALISATION AND KNOWLEDGE DIVIDE

Globalisation looks very different when it is seen, not from the capitals of the West, but from the cities and villages of the South, where most of humanity lives. Four examples taken from India, illustrate how the paradoxical forces shaping globalisation look when seen from the other side.

5 School children died in a remote village in India after drinking water and powdered milk mixed in a vat that had contained a powerful insecticide. Nobody could read the label of the vat and the children were poisoned. The insecticide in question has been banned in practically every industrialised nation; its sale continues only in places like my country.

Secondly, an important annual event recently took place in North India. Potato growers gather there to exchange the best seeds they have produced in the last year. It is an act of pride for communities to share with other's seeds that will help improve the production of potatoes. A transnational corporation attended the festival and are now working to patent the genes of these traditional foodstuffs in order to sell them as profit.

India's macro-economic indicators are excellent. In the offices of investment bankers, you will be told that India is a great investment opportunity. The situation is not so rosy, however. Thirty per cent of the population have been living below the poverty line for the last so many years. Ten per cent of the population are living below the critical poverty line: their income is insufficient to pay for even minimal nourishment. So much of the workforce is unemployed or under-employed.

A distinguished North American political scientist, Dr. Benjamin Barber, recently pointed out that in the United States democracy had degenerated into bringing one group of rascals in for four years, and then throwing them out and replacing them with another group of rascals for four years. From the perspective of the South, that looks very good! In a context where rascals manipulate elections and stay in power for fifteen or sixteen years, I would appreciate the chance to throw them out through peaceful elections every four years.

Thus, the complaints of the North are often the aspirations of the South. Progress in industrialised nations can be a threat to developing countries.

Ten years ago, in the euphoria of globalisation and the expansion of services and finance that followed the fall of the Berlin Wall, I advanced the idea that we were entering a fractured global order. Globalisation brings us into contact with one another, but it also strengthens profound divisions and fractures in terms of societies and income, and most importantly in our capacity to generate and utilise knowledge. Over the last ten years, the concentration of wealth and power has greatly increased both within and between societies.

There is a real risk of two civilisations emerging, with two ways of viewing and relating to the world: one based on the capacity to generate and utilise knowledge; the other passively receiving knowledge from abroad and deprived of the ability to modify it.

The world now faces the prospect of this Knowledge Divide becoming an unbridgeable abyss. We need the international community to return to the basic principles of international co-operation and introduce the idea that a minimum level of science and technological capability, including access to the Internet, is an absolute necessity for developing countries and should be the subject of international solidarity.

This can be achieved. However, contrary to the situation of 20 years ago, national governments are no longer the major players in the game of science and technology. Whether we like it or not, the private sector and the international community of scholars must be invited to the table with governments from the North and South to begin discussing an agenda for the mobilisation of a science and technology for development. United Nations with a mandate for the development of the sciences, has a special role to play in the revitalisation of international co-operation in this field.

THE TRUTH ABOUT GLOBAL COMPETITION—THE ECONOMIC MYTHS BEHIND GLOBALISATION

Local communities everywhere are on the front lines of what might well be characterised as World War III. It is not the nuclear confrontation between East and West—between the Soviet Union and the United States—that we once feared. It is a very different kind of conflict. There is no clash of competing military forces and the struggle is not defined by national borders. But it does involve an often violent struggle for control of physical resources and territory that is destroying lives and communities at every hand. It is a struggle between the forces and institutions of economic globalisation and the communities that are trying to reclaim control of their economic lives. It is a conflict between competing goals—economic growth to maximize profits for absentee owners versus creating healthy communities that are good places for people to live. It is a competition for the control of markets and resources between global corporations and financial markets on the one hand and locally owned businesses serving local markets on the other.

Two things of fundamental importance to each and every one of us are now very much at stake.

- Will people and communities control their local resources and economies and be able to set their own goals and priorities based on their own values and aspiration? Or will these decisions be left to global financial markets and corporations that are blind to all values save one-instant financial returns?

- Will the life sustaining resources produced by the regenerative capacities of our planet's ecosystems be equitably shared to provide for the material needs of all of us who inhabit this bountiful planet, as well as for our children and their children unto the seventh generation and beyond? Or will we allow a global economic system that is now functioning on auto-pilot beyond conscious human control to consume and destroy the ecosystem and our social fabric in its insatiable quest for money?

Economists, politicians, corporate spokespersons and the media have for years been touting the benefits of the global economy. They have called on us to support trade agreements such as the North American Free Trade Agreement (NAFTA) and the World Trade Organisation (WTO) to remove the constraints of economic borders and open to everyone the opportunities of growth and prosperity in the global economy. They have promised rich rewards for those workers and communities that become successful global competitors.

Many of the most ardent boosters of economic globalisation met earlier in the year at the annual meeting of the World Economic Forum. This Forum has for years brought together top industrialists and political figures from around the world to advance the proposition that removing tariffs and other restrictions of the free international flow of trade and money is a key to creating new economic opportunity and prosperity. It thus caused quite a stir when the Forum publicly announced that economic globalisation is producing disastrous consequences that threaten the political stability of the Western democracies. Their warning bears close examination for being one of the most honest and accurate assessments of the consequences of economic globalisation yet produced by leading advocates of the that process.

The observation is that:

- Economic globalisation is causing severe economic dislocation and social instability.
- The technological changes of the past few years have eliminated more jobs than they have created.
- The global competition "that is part and parcel of globalisation leads to winner-take-all situations; those who come out on top win big, and the losers lose even bigger."
- Higher profits no longer mean more job security and better wages. "Globalisation tends to delink the fate of the corporation from the fate of its employees."
- Unless serious corrective action is taken soon, the backlash could destabilise the Western democracies.

We don't have to go far to find examples of what they are talking about and why people are getting a bit upset as they wake up to the realities of who is winning in the ruthless competition of the global economy. The disparities between the winners and losers in the global competition are becoming more obscene with each passing day.

We are coming to realise that the extravagant promises of the advocates of the global economy are based on a number of myths that have become so deeply embedded in Western industrial culture that we have grown to accept them without examination.

- The myth that growth in GNP is a valid measure of human well-being and progress;
- The myth that free unregulated markets efficiently allocate a society's resources;
- The myth that growth in trade benefits ordinary people;

- The myth that global corporations are benevolent institutions that if freed from governmental interference will provide a clean environment for all and good jobs for the poor.

- The myth that absentee investors create local prosperity.

The Growth Myth

Our measures of growth are deeply flawed in that they are purely measures of activity in the monetised economy. Expanded use of cigarettes and alcohol increases economic output both as a direct consequence of their consumption and because of the related increase in health care needs. The need to clean up oil spills generates economic activity. Gun sales to minors generate economic activity. A divorce generates both lawyers fees and the need to buy or rent and outfit a new home increasing real estate brokerage fees and retail sales. It is now well documented that in number of other countries the quality of living of ordinary people has been declining as aggregate economic output increases.

The growth myth has another serious flaw. Since 1950, the world's economic output has increased 5 to 7 times. That growth has already increased the human burden on the planet's regenerative systems—its soils, air, water, fisheries, and forestry system—beyond what the planet can sustain. Continuing to press for economic growth beyond the planet's sustainable limits does two things. It accelerates the rate of breakdown of the earth's regenerative systems—as we see so dramatically demonstrated in the case of many ocean fisheries, and it intensifies the competition between rich and poor for the resource base that remains.

This is vividly illustrated by many of the development projects in India many funded with loans from the World Bank and other multilateral development banks—that displace the poor so that the lands and waters on which they depend for their livelihood can be converted to uses that generate higher economic returns—meaning converted to use by people who can pay more than those who are displaced.

The Myth of Free Unregulated Markets

It is almost inherent in the nature of markets that their efficient function depends on the presence of a strong government to set a framework of rules for their operation. We know that free markets create monopolies, which government must break up to maintain the conditions of competition on which market function depends.

We also know that markets only allocate efficiently when prices reflect the full and true costs of production. Yet in the absence of governmental regulation, market incentives persistently push firms to cut corners on safety, pay workers less than a living wages, and dump untreated toxic discharges into a convenient river. In our present competitive context if management does not take such measures, they are likely to be replaced by the owners or bought out by someone with less scruples who will.

The Myth of Free Trade

Many so-called trade agreements, such as the North American Free Trade Agreement (NAFTA) and the World Trade Organisation (WTO) are not really trade agreements at all. They are economic integration agreements intended to guarantee the rights of global corporations to move both goods and investments where ever they wish—free from public interference and accountability. WTO is best described as a bill of rights for global corporations.

The Myth that Economic Globalisation is Inevitable

Many of the people who claim globalisation is a consequence of inevitable historical forces are paid to promote that message by the same global corporations that have invested millions of dollars in advancing the globalisation policy agenda.

The Myth that Corporations are Benevolent Institutions

The corporation is an institutional invention specifically and internationally created to concentrate control over economic resources while shielding those who hold the resulting power from liability for the consequences of its use.

The more national economies become integrated into a seamless global economy, the further corporate power extends beyond the reach of any state and the less accountable it becomes to any human interest or institution other than a global financial system that is now best described as a gigantic legal gambling casino.

All over the world people are indeed waking up to the truth about economic globalisation and are taking steps to reclaim and rebuild their local economies. Such communities face basic choices as to how they will divide their efforts between competing for share of the declining pool of good jobs that global corporations offer and working to create locally owned enterprises that sustainably harvest and process local resources to produce the jobs and the goods and services that local people need to live healthy, happy, and fulfilling lives in balance with the environment.

Our experience with the real consequences of economic globalisation is pointing to many important lessons. One such lesson is that economies should be local, rooting power in the people and communities who realise their well-being depends on the health and vitality of their local ecosystem. If it is protectionist to favour local firms and workers who pay local taxes, live by local rules, respect and nurture the local ecosystems, compete fairly in local markets, and contribute to community life—then let us all proudly proclaim ourselves to be protectionist.

Such choices are not isolationist, to the contrary, they create a foundation for creative cooperation with our neighbours—whether they be in the United States or in other countries—to share experience, ideas, and technology—and to join in international solidarity in rewriting the rules of the global economy to favour local over global businesses, and to encourage cooperative relations among people and communities. It is our consciousness—our ways of thinking and our sense of membership in a larger community—not our economies—that should be global.

Millions of people are also making an important discovery—that life is about living—not consuming. A life of material sufficiency can be filled with social, cultural, intellectual, and spiritual abundance that place no burden on the planet.

It is time to assume responsibility for creating a new human future of just and sustainable communities freed from the myth that greed, competition, and mind-less consumption are paths to individual and collective fulfilment. It will take millions of people around the world—linked together into a powerful political coalition aimed at radical political and economic-reform to win the war that global capital is waging against us.

GLOBALISATION: A MORAL IMPERATIVE

Globalisation has become today's buzzword. It has also become a battle ground for two radically opposed groups. There are the anti-globalists, who fear globalisation and stress only its downside, seeking therefore powerful interventions aimed at taming, if not (unwittingly) crippling it. Then there are the "globalists" (a class to which I belong) who celebrate globalisation instead, emphasise its upside, while seeking only to ensure that its few rough edges be handled through appropriate policies that serve to make globalisation yet more attractive.

Many anti-globalists consider the central problem of globalisation to be its amorality, or even its immorality. But these critics too have a blanket approach to globalisation. The word covers a variety of phenomena that characterise an integrating world economy: trade, short-term capital flows, direct foreign investment, immigration, cultural convergence *et al.* The sins of one of the above cannot be visited upon the virtues of another. Some are benign even when largely unregulated whereas others can be fatal if left wholly to the marketplace.

In particular, the freeing of trade is largely benign: if I exchange some of my toothpaste for some of your toothbrushes, we will both be better of than if we did not trade at all. It would require a wild imagination, and a deranged mind, to think that such freeing of trade leads to debilitating economic crises. Equally, it is illogical to believe, as non-economists who fear globalisation do, that freeing of trade is bad because the freeing of short-term capital flows led to a debilitating financial and economic crises and could do so again. In fact, while there are some obvious simulates between free trade and free capital flows e.g. that segmentation of markets creates efficiency losses—the economic and political dissimilarities are even more compelling and policymakers cannot ignore them.

Anti-globalist critics are in fact often reacting viscerally to a much larger issue: the victory of capitalism over its arch rival, communism. For campus idealists who have always looked for alternatives to what they conventionally consider to be the greed and lack of social conscience that characterize capitalism, the situation is pyschologically intolerable. Some have turned to street theatre, nihilism and the anti-intellectualism that has been manifest in the last few years. The more sophisticated have succumbed to a stereotypical representation of corporation as the evil forces of capitalism that have captured that state, democratic institutions, and even international bodies such as the World Trade Organisation.

What these critics often forget is that certain economic freedoms are basic to prosperity and social well-being under any conditions, and are thus of the highest moral value. Property rights and markets, for instance, provide incentives to produce and allocate resources efficiently, and can in turn strengthen democracy by allowing a means of sustenance out side pervasive government structures. The quality and breadth of democracy can then be enlarged as excluded groups, such as women and the poor, are pulled into literacy, gainful employment and better health through higher public spending or the spread of economic incentives.

Critics nevertheless go on to maintain that the global spread of free markets and free trade is responsible for continuing poverty in poor countries, and for alleged growth in inequality between and within countries. Labour unions in the rich countries also fear that trade in cheap labour-using goods from poor countries.

But I do not think these concerns are well-founded. In India which has almost a quarter of the world's poor, there is good evidence that autarchic and anti-market policies produced abysmally low growth rates at 3.5 per cent annually over a quarter of a century, with a correspondingly negligible impact on poverty has declined. Higher growth rates in turn depend on several factors but openness to trade and direct investment and a skillful use of markets are definitely and important contributory factor.

As for inequality among nations, it is precisely those countries that embraced integration into the world economy, i.e. the Far Eastern Four and then the ASEAN countries, which raced ahead with dramatic growth rates whereas several countries of Africa, Latin America and Asia that looked inwards failed to deliver growth and also made little dent on poverty.

The evidence on trade and investment impoverishing our workers is also flawed. My own research suggests that the downward pressure on workers' wages due to technical change has been dampened, and magnified, by trade with the poor countries. Research also shows that big corporations use abroad technologies similar to those at home, instead of exploiting lower standards or forcing them yet lower through their financial clout.

One result of these mistaken arguments against globalisation has been an insistent clamour for certain environmental and labour standard to be linked to rules on international trade. But by seeking to create new obstacles to free trade, you undermine the freeing of trade, while mixing up trade with a moral agenda undermines that very moral agenda. It gives other countries the definite impression that you are using ethical rhetoric to mask protectionist self-interest.

The notion that global free trade and investment are responsible for poverty, inequality, lowering of standards and harming social progress is little short of astonishing. Yet national politicians and international bureaucrats give it who think that going along is way of getting along. In denying the virtues of globalisation, they actually harm the very causes they profess to embrace.

5
THE NATION STATE AND GLOBALISATION

The world has changed dramatically. Some of the changes are as yet only dimly understood. We are all going to be confronted with many challenges to the whole concept of government and to the role of the nation state as we move into the next century.

There are two principal aspects to these changes. Globalisation of the world economies is sharply limiting the independence of action of the nation state. In addition, we are only just beginning to understand what the existence of one superpower, supreme militarily, financially, means to the evolution of world diplomacy and world politics.

These remarks are directed to the first aspect. Governments are now losing influence. Private enterprise, capitalism, summarised as 'the market', is gaining power. Privatisation is a keyword. Across the political spectrum, liberal, conservative and formerly socialist parties have all accepted the downsizing of government, the privatisation of many activities and the reduction of government debt. Governments in crisis in the developed or in the developing world have been left in no doubt about what they should do.

The International Monetary Fund and the World Bank have made it clear that assistance would not be available to countries in distress unless appropriate policies were put in place, and IMF prescriptions often involve substantial and detailed micro-economic reform within a country with considerable hardship for its people.

Meanwhile, competition for international capital has become much more severe. In the early independence years, Commonwealth countries believed they could write their own international rules about the performance and behaviour of capital. Now those rules have to be rewritten to maximise international attraction. The relationship has to be competitive, the rules have to be friendly to capital. This is a totally different environment from the one in which most Commonwealth countries gained their independence in the immediate post war years.

The new global organisation of industry has significant consequences for social policy. Many governments would have conducted policies designed to see that workers gained a fair share of the returns of an enterprise. With the globalisation of industry, such policies are no longer possible. Governments now tend to argue for lower wages, for smaller workforces, to maximise the competitiveness of their particular country as a home for global corporations. This has consequences of enhancing the profit share as opposed to the wage share of a particular enterprise.

One direct consequence of these changes is a significantly growing disparity in wealth between rich and poor in all countries worldwide. This may not matter so much if the poor were also becoming better of compared to their own earlier standards but in many cases this is not so. The idea of a living wage is no longer relevant. Workers in some countries are often paid a wage which could not support even the smallest of families. In this day, if that is what the market determines, then that is what must happen.

In today's world, governments must fashion their policies to meet the wishes of the international market place. There are fundamental differences from earlier times. The global organisation of industry in which national boundaries become irrelevant is certainly new. Some aspects of information technology can operate much faster and with more devastating effect than the old cable system of the last hundred years. This has led to an explosive growth in financial markets. The volume of money traded each day is huge (and) through modern communications, this finance has great mobility.

We all know enough of markets to know that they favour the powerful, the united and the strong and that markets can overwhelm and destroy smaller players. Sometimes smaller players are entire nations.

Those who suggest that the markets alone must be allowed to determine economic outcomes favour a world in which the large will do much better than the small. So far as countries are concerned, most Commonwealth countries are in the smaller category in a world in which large financial institutions and manufacturing corporations operating globally will dominate trade and commerce.

For most countries, banks and financial institutions, which are part of the culture of that country, will become a matter of the past. Banking services will be American, European, Japanese or perhaps Chinese. The consequences of this market dominance are clear. Corporations need a global spread and many national rules of the good order and conduct of business and commerce will no longer be relevant.

For the world as a whole, the most serious problem is volatility, possibly leading to systematic breakdown. Since the Asian economic problems of 1997, there has been a great deal of discussion about the present system and about changes that need to be made.

For a while it appeared that the United States really was going to move the reform process forward but now the tendency seem to be 'it's all right, we have escaped, leave well enough alone' ...There is a need to reform the system, to establish much tougher international rules for prudential supervision and control. The IMF has demonstrated time and time again that it is not interested in avoiding crises, it is only interested in picking up the pieces after they have occurred. If this is its charter, it certainly needs reviewing. The IMF's present operations are inadequate.

Since governments have seemingly lost significant power to corporations and to financial markets and since they do operate within an increasingly globalised framework, individual governments are not capable of undertaking this task. The task is international and global. Whether it is a reformed IMF or a new institution is a matter for debate.

At their last meeting the Commonwealth Finance Ministers pointed to a number of changes, most of which are desirable, but there was no sense of great urgency, no sense of dynamism. They spoke of a need for new financial market architecture but nobody has tried to spell out what that means.

There are two specific tasks: how to preserve some form of equity and reasonable competition in a globalised market place and how to establish stability within the financial markets themselves.

The IMF's financial resources should be strengthened as a means of averting crises through the provision of contingency funds. Immediate access to adequate funding can be essential for this purpose if crises are to be avoided. Finding a way to encourage the IMF to help avert crises instead of just reacting to crises after they have occurred is a most important requirement.

In any liquidity arrangements, assisting a country in distress, the IMF should take care not to absolve lenders of their responsibility. In some cases IMF should take care not to absolve lenders of their responsibility. In some cases IMF bailouts have done more to help the lenders than the countries themselves. The lenders need to carry their own risk.

For poor countries, how to protect themselves and advance the welfare of their own people in an unpredictable world is a major challenge and very often a major problem. Apart from moves to establish greater stability designed to avoid systematic breakdown within the world's financial system, there also need to be urgent moves to establish an international body to establish rules for fair trading in a globalised environment. Middle ranking and small countries would have most to gain from such an innovation.

HIGH WORLD TRADE GROWTH VS OUTPUT—WTO SEES LINK TO GLOBALISATION

World trade in merchandise goods is expected to increase in volume by 8 per cent in 1995 down marginally on the very high 9½ per cent for 1994. Although the current outlook is for a further modest slowing next year, trade growth will remain above the average of the past decade.

Recent trade growth figures continue to exceed world production growth by a large margin in 1995 probably by a factor of almost three and next year close to double. This persistent pattern relates closely to the "globalisation" of the world economy; a process which, brings far-reaching benefits and which can be promoted through the further development of the multilateral trading system.

The recent growth is as follows:

- a 13 per cent rise pushed the value of world merchandise trade past the $ 4,000 billion mark for the first time, to $ 4,090 billion;
- an 8 per cent increase in the value of trade in commercial services, to $ 1,100 billion, after near stagnation in 1993;
- a 23 per cent increase in the dollar value of merchandise trade in the first six months of 1995

which, allowing for the depreciation of the US dollar, is consistent with a full-year growth in trade volume of 8 per cent.

Globalisation

Over the period from 1950 (when the process of trade liberalisation through the early GATT Round got under-way) to 1994, the volume of world merchandise trade increased at an annual rate of slightly more than 6 per cent and world output by close to 4 per cent. Thus, during those 45 years world merchandise trade multiplied 14 times and output 5½ times. However, the excess of trade growth over output growth varied; from an average of a mere half percentage point in the period 1974-84 to nearly 3½ percentage points in the most recent 10 years. In fact, the excess during the years since 1990 has been much higher still but it is not yet clear whether or not this represents a permanent shift to a faster rate of increase in the world's trade-to-output ratio.

To the question "will globalisation continue?" In this regard one has to observe two factors—technological change and the evolving strategies of firms and individual investors—impart a natural momentum to global integration. It is government policies which can speed-up, slow down or even reverse progress on global integration. It this context, the role of non-discrimination—in particular, through the "most-favoured-nation" (MFN) clause-is examined.

The MFN Clause

MFN was the centrepiece of a multiplicity of bilateral trade agreements reached in Europe in the second half of the 19th century, a period marked by very low tariffs and rapidly increasing trade. In contrast, the 1920s and the 1930s saw efforts to restore liberal trade through international trade conferences rather than legally-binding commercial treaties based on MFN. The failure of these efforts contributed to the Great Depression and provided some of the roots of military confrontation in 1939. It was only after the War that negotiations established what become the GATT, a multilateral contract consisting of rules and disciplines and based firmly (Article) on MFN treatment.

The GATT system has been a post-war bulwark against a return to the trade chaos of the 1930's. In the 1990's, a disintegration of the globalised international economy on the scale of the 1930's is almost unthinkable. In contrast, today "the threat that would be posed by a loss of credibility of the multilateral rules" (now represented by the WTO) would be "a fracturing of the global economy into inward-looking and potentially antagonistic trading blocs".

One can suggest two safeguards against such an eventuality:

- the examination of new ways to ensure that free-trade areas and customs unions remain outward-looking and complement rather than compete with the multilateral trading system; and

- progress in dealing, at the multilateral level, with new issues tied directly to the further evolution of the global economy. These include telecommunications, financial services, environment, competition and investment policies among others.

Progress in dealing with these and other issues at the multilateral level will have a significant impact on the future pace of global integration, both directly and through its impact on the credibility of the multilateral system in influencing the broad spectrum of national trade policies.

7

URBANISATION AND GLOBALISATION

How we handle globalisation will determine whether our cities and our civilisation will be divided and violent or user-friendly and peaceful. We cannot get a clear picture of urban life in the 21st century, especially in the poor countries of the South, unless we take into account the phenomenon of globalisation, which has already brought dramatic changes make their first appearance. So it is there too that the great upheavals of the next century will take place.

Globalisation gives shape to the "Global Village". The "information era" that it ushers in compresses time and we are now living in a world speeded up as never before. World-wide urbanisation is proceeding at a similar rate and its pace in the poor countries of the South seems terrifying. By 2025, two-thirds of humanity will be living in cities and towns, where the best opportunities in life tend to be.

Globalisation also accentuates a "new urban geography" in both North and South. Islands of rich consumers are springing up in cities amid an ocean of deprived people. More and more unemployed people, immigrants, minorities and the homeless, are pushed into cities by pressure from "market economies". As a result, all urban areas—not just those in the poor countries of the South—will have a deal with growing internal tensions. In New York, for example, the poorest 20 per cent of the population earns 15 times less than the richest 20 per cent.

Cities have always had their smart neighbourhoods and their dangerous areas. But such social and geographical segregation has changed in pace and scale because of the growth in the urban population, the increase in "illegal' migrants and rising uncertainty.

In fact, we have entered a period of historical transition, where discontinuities prevail over adjustment. Radical changes in the nature of production and jobs and the incredible concentration of capital in the hands of the financial sector and speculators weigh much heavier in our lives these days than the state's efforts to adjust and improve the market economy. Segregation in cities has given a new lease of life whose consequences we do not know. It has reached unprecedented dimensions because of the explosive growth of urban areas.

According to one scenario, things will go badly. The growing pace of globalisation will increase uncertainty about the future. Fear and defence mechanisms will grow among people and institutions, fuelling intolerance, xenophobia and mistrust of everything new or foreign. Urban tensions will manifest themselves with increasing violence, and segregation will sharpen. Public areas will be abandoned and become dangerous no-man's-lands, the wretched abode of society's rejects. Cities will lose their original function of being a crossroads for meeting and exchange.

If globalisation also continues to go hand in hand with deregulation of financial markets and an unchanged level of indebtedness of poor countries, the latter will not be able to maintain their urban infrastructures. And if on top of this there is corruption and lack of political will, challenges to the system will increase and violence will grow. Cash-strapped authorities will respond with undemocratic mafias which provide them with funds.

According to a second scenario, everything will be all right. In line with the principle that "everything the state does is public, but the state doesn't control everything that is public," a new social contract will be drawn up between the state, the market, the working population and civil society, including NGOs. Cities will develop a new quality of life by providing citizens with forum for exchange. Jobs will be created in the social sector, in the fields of the environment, education, research, culture and leisure, opening up possibilities for young people.

In the countries of the South, long-term development strategies will be drafted and urban planning practised, taking advantage of the opportunities provided by globalisation but without falling into its traps. Town planning will become part of the political process, and the state will work with the private sector, monitored by institutions of civil society. Adequate housing will be built with the help of microcredit and controls on the price of building materials. Improved infrastructures will enable marginal areas to become part of the civilized part of the city. Democracy will come up with new ways of governing with the help of networks of involved citizens.

In a transitional scenario, action strategies should fall somewhere between these two extremes. They should include social goals so that in big urban areas a society emerges which is founded on participatory democracy and on "capitalism with a human face" or "market socialism".

But the outlook is less clear than ever. Let us hope the present transition will lead rapidly to a new revival of humanism, whose first signs we are already seeing. This wouid open up the road to a development which is fair, humane and peaceful.

MYTHS AND ILLUSIONS

The tide of precarity is rising steadily, so that people who have never been poor no longer regard poverty as a distant prospect but as one so close that it could engulf them at any moment.

In 1989, the fall of the Berlin Wall was rightly welcomed because it marked the collapse of a system that provided a degree of equality but rejected freedom. Today there is a strong possibility that the system gradually spreading all over the world—a kind of neo-liberal fundamentalism—may also collapse. In its obsession with freedom, vital though freedom is, this fundamentalism disregards equality, a term which should not be regarded here in purely static and statistical terms, but as something dynamic and ethical. Equality can only be truly practised in a context of social solidarity or to borrow from the vocabulary of the French Revolution of fraternity.

On the one hand, we have a world that is immensely rich in resources, possibilities, knowledge and experience; its consistuent societies are freer and more dynamic than ever. There is an extraordinary potential for everyone to live a better life. But at the same time, new and ever higher walls are being built both between peoples and between social groups within individual countries. We are experiencing a travesty of development, which is creating a world bipolarized into extremes of wealth and poverty.

The most common reactions to this disastrous situation are very often the result of two misapprehensions. The first can only be described as ideological or doctrinaire since it is not based on the facts as they can be observed. It says that since the dominant system of values and things is by definition more than satisfactory, the persistence of impoverishment is merely a temporary blip. Enough time has elapsed, however, for us to see that this is not the case, including in countries where this system has been part of the established order for more than a century. One statistic is particularly eloquent. In just over 30 years, world production has approximately doubled, but the gap has more than doubled between the income of the 20 per cent of world's people living in the richest countries and the income of the world's poorest 20 per cent, according to the United Nations Development Programme.

The second misapprehension stems from another form of blindness and illusion, namely the belief that poverty can be regarded exclusively as a moral issue, as if it had no other kind of implications for those who are not poor. Globalisation is, however, a two-way process. It enable the countries of the North to export their values and their paradigms as well as their goods and capital to the countries of the South, but it also makes them much more vulnerable to the backlash of crises that afflict these countries. Even in the North, the cult of competitiveness is undermining situations once considered extremely stable. The tide of precarity is rising steadily, so that people who have never been poor no longer regard poverty as a distant prospect but as one so close that it could engulf them at any moment.

Because of inadequate socio-economic development, the extraordinary upsurge of democracy over the past 30 years remains a very fragile process, and there is a risk that the trend may be reversed. When hunger, disease and ignorance prevail, citizens' participation in decision-making becomes either non-existent or a more charade. Democratic institutions become empty shells, representational bodies existing in form only and devoid of real significance.

Social division caused by economic distortions exacerbate the failures of democracy which in turn pose serious threats to civil order within countries and to peace between nations. It is high time to face these obvious facts.

DEMOCRACY AND THE MARKET ECONOMY

Today the idea of democracy is triumphant; the model is in principle embraced in most countries the world over. You may say that the very word democracy has been hailed and misused earlier in history. The most repressing and totalitarian regimes have tried to mask themselves as 'real' or 'peoples' democracies. What has happened, however, is a historical demasking of these false pretences.

What exactly do we mean by democracy? There is now a general agreement that democracy cannot be defined by purpose of policy or levels of mass mobilisation. It must be defined as a political system where different parties or individuals compete for power through regular free elections where all adult citizens have a vote. Moreover, a democracy must uphold certain basic human rights and well-defined freedoms which make the political process possible, and respect the opinion and integrity of the individual. No other definitions hold, and we should be careful when we talk about "real" democracy versus "formal" democracy. A society which in real life upholds the constitutional or formal democratic principles and which in practice applies the rights these principles imply, is by definition a democracy. A society with a beautiful-sounding constitution but where none or few of these rights are respected is certainly not a democracy.

Democratic Government no Guarantee for Equality

It is important to understand that democratic government does not necessarily mean good government in the sense that those in power make wise or well-considered decisions. Nor does it mean that conflicts inherent in the society are reduced to a minimum. Demands for democracy, social justice and a better life have historically gone hand in hand, but this does not mean that the establishment of a democratic system actually does lead to an improvement in social conditions or equality. It is also quite clear that some societies have a sort of outer shell of democracy but in reality, exclude large groups of people from having any political influence whatsoever. The actual differences in living conditions are so enormous and so entrenched that these people have no confidence at all in the political system even if it is democratic according to the definition. In these cases—for example in some Latin American countries—one can talk of a "masked hegemony with competing elities" where the outcome of struggles for power has little relevance for the masses. It is a sort of social and political half-authoritarian system—but disguised as a democracy—where the military often have a significant influence.

In the rhetoric of the day the terms market economy and democracy are used as if they were synonymous or atleast naturally emerging at the same time. But this is wrong—or atleast misleading. When the market economy or capitalism finally established itself in the 1800s and came to characterize modern industrial civilisation, democracy was at best in its infancy. In fact one could argue that democracy grew out of the contradictions and social dynamism inherent in the market economy of the capitalistic system. In this century we have a long list of terrifying and repressive regimes which have nevertheless upheld the virtues of a market economy. That some of these regimes have for ideological and security reason been hailed as bastions against communism, and also dignified members of the so-called free world does not transform them into democracies. In this company it is perhaps unnecessary to remind ourselves that the colonial system as assuredly not democratic, but was certainly based on capitalistic or market economic principles. It is the sad but irrefutable historical coupling between Western democracy, colonialism, and the plundering of resources in the name of the market economy which for understandable reasons meant that many of the leaders of national liberation movements looked for other models for the development of their young nations. In this connection it can be worth remembering what Nelson Mendela said soon after his release from 26 years of prison in the market economic but racist state of South Africa. "When we in ANC during 40 years struggle for democracy we were put in prison by the same people who are now telling us how we should behave to promote the democracy we have been rejected by all these years".

While we can see that a market economy does not automatically lead to democracy, a functioning democracy—as we have defined it—does seem to require some form of free economic system.

Democracy and Economic Freedom

Theoretically, it is conceivable that a political democracy could be combined with an economy totally controlled by the government—but experience has shown this to be very difficult. One could even argue that it is by definition impossible since democracy implies a certain freedom of economic choice and independent economic factors. A functioning democratic system presupposes what is now often referred to as a civil society—in practice, independent institutions, companies, organisations, the media etc., regulated by law but not subject to or controlled by those in power.

We must also see clearly that there are no unambiguous relations between economic growth, development and democracy. Democratic governments are neither very successful when it comes to structural reforms which may be to the disadvantage of important interests in the society, nor when it comes to welfare. The developing countries which have achieved the greatest success economically and socially over the last 20 years are the East Asian countries—which all have had various kinds of more are less authoritarian systems.

However, that does not mean that you can use these countries as models for the rest of the world. There is no globally valid link between an authoritarian form of regime and economic development, not even when development is defined only in terms of autocentric growth. Many social scientists—have tried to find some systematic connection between what we call development or modernisation on the one hand, and the political system on the other—but all have failed.

It is also obvious that one of several pre-requisites for economic growth and development is legitimate and reasonably well functioning government and governance. If the free market is to be a motor for development and improved welfare, and not just a meeting place for robber barons, the Mafia and speculators, you must have a regulating and supportive state. If economic history teaches us anything, it is just this. Consider the astounding development in Germany after the war, or in Japan and the other East Asian countries some years later. There are many differences, but what they have in common is a well-functioning government apparatus with a long tradition.

Today we find ourselves in a historical situation where a large number of countries in the former communist states of Europe, in Africa, Asia and Latin America are at one and the same time trying to establish a new democratic system and new economic mechanisms. The situation is unique, and the intrinsic problems are unprecedented. Democracy as an idea has triumphed but in its practice it is in profound trouble. It is no exaggeration to talk of the crisis of democracy.

The former communist countries are certainly in crisis. As a by-product of the past regimes, there is an intensive suspicion of the political institutions, of the state and the parties—and in this way also the legitimacy of democracy and the ability of the politicians to deal with the fundamental problems of society has been undermined. The lack of a democratic tradition is not overcome from one day to the next.

Many of the developing countries have similar difficulties. The introduction of a multiparty system does not in itself mean that one can manage the conflicts and social problems in a democratic way.

Countries in Transition

Both in the East and the South countries are trying, at one and the same time, to change the political and economic system. When the whole society is convulsed by economic changes, and where peoples' living conditions fundamentally change, it is not easy to develop and maintain a political system based on compromise and respect, including respect for minorities.

As in previous history the deep crises of ligitimacy and general frustration feed national and ethnical conflicts. These conflicts establish themselves in societies where the authoritarian system, economic crises and the breakdown of traditional values rob people of any kind of kinship other than ethnical.

We cannot avoid seeing disturbing signs of this crisis of democracy also in the so-called "established democracies" of the rich countries.

It is obvious that the state of democracy varies from country to country, as do the reason for a feeling of dejection. But there are some similarities too.

The continuing and noticeable internationalisation limits the national freedom of political choice, available alternatives, and makes it more difficult for people to see the connection between 'politics' and their actual living conditions. The governments are restrained by international economic events. The reaction of the stock exchange may be more important than that of the voters. The election results influence the stock exchange prices—but is it perhaps not also so that the stock exchanges, indirectly, also influence the election results? People feel themselves to be the victims of major economic changes, but no one seems to be responsible and they themselves feel they have little chance of influencing the outcome. The absence of clearly identifiable alternatives between the larger political parties provides opportunities for the populist and the extremists.

There is indeed reason to reflect on the lessons of the history of our turbulent and cruel century.

Priority for Growth

There is today much concern about the lack of resources for such urgent needs as the reconstruction of the East, a concerted attack on poverty and human development in the poorest countries, and environmental investments of all kinds. If the growth of world output returns to the levels of the 1980s, total output would grow by about one trillion dollars a year. There is, infact, on other way to resolve the economic and political crises multiplying in the world community than to give priority to the restoration of growth.

We are certainly not at the end of history as someone has argued. We are rather at a dramatic turning point, a moment of many possibilities and many dangers. What we do now, for a few years ahead, may direct the future for several decades—like the dramatic and fateful years immediately after the second world war. All nations, all governments, have a responsibility. The rich world has a special responsibility, not just moral because of its enormous economic and political power.

10
WHAT WAS WRONG WITH STRUCTURAL ADJUSTMENT

In defence of a Much-Maligned Strategy

After decades of stranded development theories, ideologies and paradigms, "structural adjustment", with its demands for clean fiscal policy and an end to uneconomic state enterprises, political privileges, market and exchange rate intervention and corruption, entered the aid arena like a refreshing dawn after a long night of frustrating dreams. Only the "old guard" of planned economy advocates and jealous academicians who had missed the boat were able to shut their eyes to the moral and economic justification of this liberating breakthrough in international development policy spearheaded by the Breton Woods institutions then steered by some exceptionally courageous economists.

Reaction to Saps

As the with any revolution, defeat is awaiting the pioneers at the hands of political power greed, reactionary tactics by the formerly privileged and academic envy. The principal device serving the reactionary forces as a lever of influence on the mood of the "development community" has been the identification and dramatisation of new pockets or strata of (principally urban) poverty allegedly created by structural adjustment measures, while shunning the much broader-based rise in economic activity, real incomes and sense of fair reward in the overall society, especially the rural population. That the hardship experienced by urban poor, formerly privileged under consumer price control and import subsidies to the debit of depressed farm prices or maintained by grossly over-expanded public payrolls, was only laying open the camouflaged erosion of the economy and near-bankruptcy of governments and public enterprises was conveniently downplayed.

These reactionary howls were to be expected. Not that they met the entirely innocent. There had been naively sweeping, overly assuming demands by some structural adjustment missions. But an intellectually vigorous and dynamic "development community" would have coped with the ensuing opposition, strengthened the analytical and monitoring capacities and the political will to endure also rocky roads and bitter medicines on the way to a healthier base. Instead, institutional rivalry, political opportunism and emotive populism were thriving. In a way, the "development community" behaved as if it did not want its patient to become able to become able to stand on his own feet and eventually steal its raison d'être.

Worst, the Bretton Woods institutions themselves, partly under the pressure of the emotive opposition described above fell to the temptation to rescue their lending volume, which was threatened by the frugality dictated to third World public budgets under structural adjustment recipes, through hardship-easing loans. They thereby corrupted their creation in using it to reinforce their indispensability. As a consequence it soon turned out that some of the most obedient loan takers under structural adjustment terms experienced sharply rising indebtedness, exploited as a disqualifying symptom by the antistructural adjustment camp.

Whatever the opinions on structural adjustment policies, the commitment to the principles of "good governance" has come to stay, at least on paper, as an almost standard conditionally for official development aid from OECD donor countries. The realisation, matured in the implementation of structural adjustment programmes, that not the quantity of aid, but the quality of Third World governments determines the positive or negative course of development, may be regarded as the most valuable fruit of the decades-old-policy debate in the 'development community". And the use of aid as a pressure or bribing factor towards "good governance" as foreign aid's least disputable purpose.

Out of the Limelight

Nothing, however, must be taken for granted. Achievement breeds its challenge! Structural adjustment, though in essence hardly disputable has been pushed out of the limelight and replaced by the oldest actor in the company: eradication of poverty, twinned with a equally perpetual endeavour at the macro-level: debt-forgiveness. This falling back to square one in donors' approach to the problems of the south, i.e., the call to alleviate poverty and priorities direct efforts to this end above all other developmental efforts—does it indicate a sell-out of constructive ideas in the 'development community"? Has any noteworthy progress been achieved in the past by this approach?

By telling a frugally toiling but independent subsistence farmer that internationally his condition is classed as 'poverty', deserving compassion and support by the world community and cancellation of his debts, one can hardly expect a sustainable improvement in his output, satisfaction, or self-respect and even less, when he realises that the help principally provides jobs, fringe benefits and self—importance to a gamut of intermediaries, at home and abroad.

What do those poverty advocates (the "Lords of poverty") really know about the resources, life management, value systems and ambitions of those they generalise by the billions? The great variance in the conception of life situations, from different external viewpoints.

What the aid system can do for these rural populations classed as 'poor'/'underprivileged'/'exploited', is press for justice, i.e., 'good governance'. The achievements of structural adjustment policy through e.g., abolishing official price and exchange rate distortions, import subsidies and exploitative state agencies, has brought massive income improvement for peasant populations, i.e., the majority of LDC inhabitants, in dimensions unreachable by whatsoever direct 'attack' on rural 'poverty'. What people want is not being benevolently treated as poor, but being justly rewarded for their work, i.e., by access to the unmanipulated market value of their output. Slackening on structural adjustment/'good governance' conditionally under the present '10 year itch' for paradigm change means foregoing much of the potential opportunities for undoing injustice and exploitation of the masses. It should be clear where priority focus should be placed in ODA policy.

Small is Not Beautiful

The direct attack on 'poverty', orchestrated by the Bretton Woods institutions under their freshly launched Poverty Reduction Strategy Paper (PRSP) campaign, is being rightly regarded as primarily an NGO domain, since most activities are expected to be carried out at local community level. This would require careful screening and coordinating of NGO activities and their integration via gradual expansion of their experience. But 'small' is not 'beautiful' for the development financing institutions. Disbursement needs are pressing, calling for the new paradigm to quickly provide channels for another wave of loans to the 'IDA Countries'. Their problem of heavy indebtedness, which would principally exclude most of them from any new loan consideration, shall be solved with one stroke (which only the well-cushioned development bureaucracy can afford); debt relief against presentation of country PRSPs by the respective governments. NGOs are expected to play in the system especially the knowledge gap about the 'poor' people's real wants and needs NGOs will naturally be tempted by such expansionary boost to their involvement (referred to sarcastically as their philanthropic empire" by an African conference participant), but this will not be conducive to quality and accountability of their performance, which ideally should be based on privat sponsorship combination with strong target-group provided self-help components.

Patience and Self-restraint

Local knowledge and initiatives cannot be obtained under time pressure. "The grass does not grow faster by being pulled". When will the "development community" learn patience and self-restraint in the approach to LDC's capacity for constructive absorption of aid programmes accompanied by a genuine sense of ownership?

After all these deliberations, how shall development policy by shaped in order to better correspond with reality, without sinking deeper into hypocrisy and frustration?

To come back to the opening question: what has wrong with "structural adjustment"? Nothing was wrong with its intent. In fact this was very right and long overdue. Its implementation, however, lacked patience, perseverance and solid support from the development community, apart from its being corrupted as a vehicle for expansionary lending policy. If aid is meant to not be an end in itself, then structural adjustment policy needs constant reinforcement, underpinned by strict lending discipline. There should be an end to irresponsible lending and easy escape from its consequences by wholesome periodic debt relief burdened on the international tax-paying community. No ODA, either loans or grants, should be made available to governments who are not in active process of implementing "good governance" principles. A monitoring unit, reporting to the donor community on government performance in regard to its "—good government"? Structural adjustment commitment, should be maintained in each and receiving country by 'donor consortia' comprising all locally represented bilateral and multilateral development organisations currently extending technical, financial or material assistance to the country.

In order to accommodate the poverty focus without diluting the necessary structural adjustment orientation of

ODA, a division of activity-focus between the latter and the NGO sector would seem to be advantageous.

- ODA, limited to the countries abiding to structural adjustment/'good governance' conditionally, with focus concentration on sustainable physical, social and economic infrastructure principally at national and regional level, public management training, higher education and research, consultant and senior adviser services

- the NGO sector, principally funded by private sponsorship, united to structural adjustment conditioinally (but preferably grafted on local self-help initiative), with focus-concentration on the "third World "poor", i.e., mostly at rural community and low-income township level, for amelioration of living conditions and local resource utilisation.

- strengthening of linkages between the NGO sector and the UN Technical Agencies to mutual benefit: NGOs in need of professional information, evaluation and advice or forum for discussion to find an actively supportive window at the agencies; the latter to maintain and develop field contact for research and policy generation, not least as a substitute for their declining project work (giving way to greater concentration on their global functions i.e., serving as information policy initiation, and coordination/ negotiation centre on topics global concern, such as e.g.: human rights, global monetary and trade systems, tropical forest and global marine resources, global and Regional health threats, international standards.)

In conclusion, it may be called to mind that aid and its institutions have no claim for permanence. They are justified only as temporary functions in a phasing-out process of self-help support. Any claim for unlimited continuity would breed lasting infantilisation.

11

ADD VALUE, GO GLOBAL

Can Southern Firms Break into Export Markets?

The global economy has changed beyond recognition over the last decade. Widespread economic policy reform and in particular trade liberalisation have opened up new opportunities for developing countries. In poor countries, however, the consequences of trade liberalisation are not always positive. What can the private sector do to respond better and make the most of new trading opportunities? What factors have limited the impact of economic reforms on export performance?

Why have exports from poorer countries failed to increase more rapidly following trade liberalisation? What can be done to improve performance? Research on the response of firms in the private sector to economic reform can underpin new approaches to export promotion for poorer developing countries. For a long time, protective trade policies, poorly performing state-owned industries and state controls over the private sector were blamed for poor export performance in Africa and south Asia. Now that some of these problems have been remedied, other obstacles have come to light.

The effect of economic liberalisation and adjustment on the performance of poor countries has been cause for concern. Trade liberalisation should increase incentives to export and facilitate business enterprise by encouraging private ownership through privatisation and by attracting foreign investment.

Macro-economic stability ought to boost business confidence and performance. All these factors should promote exports, offsetting job and income losses caused by the closure or reorganisation of inefficient enterprises and industries yet, although some degree of reform and stability it is without export growth that was expected.

Trade reform and macro-economic stability may be necessary conditions for improved export performance but by them are insufficient. The obstacles to improving export performance are numerous and there is no easy policy answer. The research programme examined export performance at three levels.

- ***Regional:*** how trade strategies should vary with skills and natural resource endowments
- ***National:*** factors influencing the export performance of manufacturing
- ***Sectoral:*** the performance of particular sectors of the economy.

The East Asian economies have shown that developing countries can complete successfully in global markets. For many, they provide a blueprint for economic growth applicable to many poor countries.

South Asia's comparative advantage lies in its abundant unskilled labour, while Africa's lies in its abundant natural resources. Different export promotion strategies are essential. South Asia's best prospects are in labour-intensive manufacturing: the region's low level of exports would soar over the next decade if current obstacles to trade were reduced. Africa's exports could also increase but its biggest potential in primary products that need little educated labour and abundant natural resources.

Some African countries could also be substantial exporters of manufacturers, but their actual manufactured exports in most cases now fall far short. Comparing Ghana to Mauritius—one of Africa's most successful exporters of manufactured goods differences in firm-level efficiency are apparent Mauritian firms have more capital per worker and use it more efficiently. Reducing trade barriers is not sufficient. Wages in Ghana would have to be substantially lower to offset low labour productivity. Alternatively, labour productivity will have to be drastically improved in Ghanian firms are to compete successfully in export markets with wages at current levels.

Even when companies use capital and labour efficiently, poor infrastructure is a frequent stumbling products to export markets—an acute problem in landlocked countries and equally acute for manufacturers as research on Uganda clearly shows. What huts manufacturing exporters is being hit by the high cost of transporting their output to foreign markets and of transporting the materials they need from abroad. The cost penalties resulting from geography and poor infrastructure are far greater in Uganda than from high tariffs and other import restrictions.

Southern firms can still break into export markets, however, developing-country firms do export to markets with exacting standards for product quality, reliability of delivery, and consumer safety. Two crucial aspects, however, are often overlooked:

- Non-manufacturing sectors, such as tourism and horticulture, generate significant employment and offer opportunities for supplying increasingly sophisticated products. Although manufacturing is considered more attractive, certain areas of tourism and horticulture can be equally appealing.
- New export opportunities are created as southern producers establish closer links with foreign customers. Producers of labour-intensive products such as garments, horticulture and footwear frequently depend on large retailers and specialist international traders for designs, information about demand and technical support.

Supermarkets make key decisions about which fruit and vegetables to grow, how they should be produced and processed and which firms should be included in the business. Strategic decisions by international producers and retailers in the footwear industry have been crucial in developing new production locations such as Vietnam and Romania. Similarly, work on automotive components production in South Africa and India illustrates how global sourcing by the leading motor companies closes off some markets and opens up others. Export prospects can only be evaluated in the light of global restructuring in these industries.

Emphasising global linkages does not mean that developing countries are powerless in the face of global forces. Even in tightly structured industries, there is scope for national policy and national strategy. Further more, there are important export sectors that are not structured in this way. Some tourism is dominated by large northern firms and is heavily import-dependent, but there is also enormous potential and national policy will be crucial in shaping the industry and its contribution to the economy as a whole.

For southern firms to break into export markets, certain issues must be addressed, especially in Africa. Some are recognised as important policy issues—investing in human capital and improving infrastructure for example. As one set of constraints are reduced—such as removing policy—induced distortions through trade liberalisation—another set takes precedence. In response to the integration of global markets, southern producers must join the global distribution chains to ensure markets for their exports.

These findings impose hard choices on developing countries. Should a firm allocate limited funds for investment in human capital or investment infrastructure? Future research might contribute by quantifying relative rates of return. On another level, countries may worry about the independence and autonomy of local producers if they are to join a global chain typically donated by northern companies. Rules regulate governmental trade and investment policies but who controls the global buyers and multinational companies whose decisions have such huge impacts on developing countries?

12
RENEWING THE STATE

Many view globalisation as a technology driven global order that has led to an intensification of interconnectedness among nations. This, however, is merely one fact of globalisation, and does not presuppose the ideological homogenization or the rapid retrenchment of the welfare state that is currently underway.

The dispute over globalisation is not about the intensification of global interconnectedness. Rather, it is over the vision of the global system that globalisation projects. This vision entails a global economic system with indentifiable rules of behaviour in trade, finance, taxation, investment policy, intellectual property rights, and currency convertibility, all of which are crafted along neo-liberal principles with minimal governmental regulation. This global system represents a new phase of capitalism which is "more universal, more unchallenged, more pure and more unadulterated than even before".

For many critics, globalisation is essentially an anti-democratic process that excludes the interest of a wide range of groups. But the process is not shaped by market forces alone. It is only made possible by the acquiescence if not active support of governments, especially those in advanced countries.

Governments in devolving countries, meanwhile, are often said to be unable to stand up to globalisation without incurring severe costs. The Government of South Africa, for example, could be punished by capital flight if it insists on implementing its agenda of social reform. The masses of South Africa, however, are likely to sustain heavier costs if the government abandons its reforming mandate. Faced with such a dilemma, governments have generally selected the side of capital for a simple reason.

The list of problems caused by globalisation is long. In low-income countries, such as those in Sub-Saharan Africa, where governments have been unable or unwilling to provide their populations with even the most basic protection from the new phase of global capitalism and structural adjustment programmes, the people's plight has been particularly severe.

Opponents of globalisation are addressing genuine problems. But it is uncertain whether they will succeed in reversing globalisation or even in mitigating its adverse impacts. To begin with, many of them are badly organised. Most of them have also rallied around specific issues instead of articulating a comprehensive counter vision. At this point, the counter vision they project appears to be a global system which is not shaped by the narrow interests of capital but which accommodates the interests of diverse social groups. This vision, however, is not yet well developed.

Further more, these opponents have yet to develop viable strategies to constrain globalisation. Some argue for weakening or even abolishing institutions such as the World Bank, the International Monetary Fund, and the World Trade Organisation, which they view as agents of globalisation, it is unclear why business interests and governments would allow this to happen. The relevance of these bodies is only likely to decline if Third World countries, especially middle-income ones, begin to reduce their dependence of them under pressure from their populations.

Yet the main problem faced by these critics is that many of them do not see the relevance of the state. A successful struggle for genuine popular democracy can liberate the state from the grip of corporate and financial interest, turning it into a critical agent for the promotion of broad social interests. Many NGOs rely instead of civil society, though this cannot substitute the state in policymaking. The struggle against globalisation is essentially a struggle for democracy; the state cannot be bypassed, but must be won.

13

TAKING A LEAD IN THE FIGHT AGAINST POVERTY?

World Bank and IMF Speed Implementation of Their New Strategy

A change in development policy strategy in the poorest countries is at present being prepared with incredible speed. The IMF-style structural adjustment programmes that have been criticised for many years are being scrapped,. The countries are now to take their own decision on their paths to development. Their governments will no longer formulate poverty reduction programmes top-down, but in an intensive and long-term dialogue with societal groups and organisations. Governments and institutions of the North commit themselves to supporting these processes, such as by debt relief on an unprecedented scale. Dream or reality?

New Strategy Paper

Behind this euphoria lines a new abbreviation, PRSP, standing for Poverty Reduction Strategy Paper, which the IMF and World Bank invented last year. The G-7 countries in Cologne not only announced debt relief for the Heavily Indebted Poor Countries (HIPCs) but also demanded that it must serve above all for poverty reduction. The PRSP concept was then presented at the annual conference of the two Bretton Woods organisations.

The most important principles of the new 'super weapon' in the fight against poverty are:

- PRSPs are papers, which describe the medium-term development paths of the poorest countries of the South, particularly their strategies to combat poverty, and by this means enlist international support. A PRSP is not only the prerequisite for granting debt forgiveness in the context of the HIPC initiative. It is also necessary for all new IMF and World Bank loans to the so-called IDA countries, the some 70 poorest countries that receive concessional loans from the World Bank's International Development Agency (IDA). According to the World Bank, PRSPs should also be required for all future pledges of bilateral development assistance.

- Not only social sector programmes, but also the economic and financial policies of the developing countries are in future to be aimed at fighting poverty. Previously, the IMF always pronounced that a growth-oriented national economy and a far-reaching integration in the world market would have a trickle-down effect and also benefit the poor. Now the poor are to be asked what policies can help materially to improve their situation.

- PRSPs are to be developed on the basis of self-responsible country ownership. Accordingly, development and structural adjustment strategies are no longer to be developed by the Washington finance institutions, but the countries themselves.

- The heading "country ownership" is to underline that not only governments are called upon, PRSPs should come into being in a participatory process. That means involvement of trade unions, NGOs, cooperatives, associations, grass roots, groups, political parties and parliaments. A country's PRSP should be developed in a societal debate, a dialogue between governments on one side and parliamentary, private sector and civil society on the other.

Rhetoric or Reality?

Are PRSPs the expression of a change of paradigm? In brief, if all what the papers contain is implemented in a consistent and wide-ranging, way, the chances of a achieving it are good but there are a number of open questions. The answers to them will have a bearing on success or failure.

- Is the IMF really changing its policy on the poorest countries or merely wrapping its old policy in new words? The growing criticism of the IMF in recent years strengthened latterly by the evaluation of the ESAF (Enhanced Structural Adjustment Facility) programmes, which once again proved their blatant weaknesses called for reaction and is now triggering changes—real or only rhetorical? There will be no more old-style ESAF loans based on macro-economic structural adjustment programmes. But the credit line remains, and is now called the Poverty Reduction and Growth Facility (PRGF). This will be granted on the basis of the PRSPs, which in each case must also be accepted by the IMF board of directors. How much influence will the IMF have on the design of the PRSPs? What happens if a government choose macro-economic strategies combat poverty which go against previous IMF policy? Open questions. Moreover, there is still no answer to the question of why the IMF is at all coming on with long-term and low-interest lines of credit in poorest countries.

Mixed Feelings with Regard to World Bank Role

- Will the World Bank use the PRSP process to expand its own institutional power further? NGOs in the North and South are viewing this with mixed feelings. Many welcome the fact that for the moment the World Bank appears to be asserting itself against its twin, the IMF. On the other hand, 50 years of experience with World Bank strategies have certainly not strengthened their trust in the Bank's ability to make a convincing fight against poverty. That is why the EURODAD network also questions the role of the World Bank (and the IMF) in the PRSP process. It says the papers should not be presented to the two financial institutions, whose power over the development strategies of countries of the South thus would increase further. Rather, PRSPs should for example, be laid before a Round Table of all donors chaired by the United Nations Development Programme (UNDP).

Ownership

- The principles of developing countries being responsible for their own development strategies are as old as it is—in theory—right. There have been frequent complaints about shortcomings in ownership. But now, after decades of development strategies being set and structural adjustment programmes being dictated from outside, the governments of the poorest countries, which in many cases have only weak institutional capacities, can hardly taken on responsibility overnight. In addition, of course, not a few of the countries are ruled by corrupt political elites (promoted from outside over decades) that give little reason to hope they would immediately switch to poverty reduction politics. Scepticism and critical observation is justified even if there is no alternative to governments of the south taking other greater responsibility.

- Civil society actors are now asked to help out in particular in those countries whose governments appear to be less trustworthy. A nice idea that has little to do with real life. Civil society actors in developing countries in general and in the poorest countries in particular are extraordinarily weak institutions which in many cases are totally dependent on financing from the North.

The civil society landscape in other countries is even weaker. However, some actors in many countries could make useful contributions to developing sustainable strategies. But that calls for meaningful and lasting support, including financial support, capacity-building, and in some countries also political pressure to gain scope for societal engagement.

It is reasonable that not only the World Bank and other official donors but also, and above all, the northern NGO partners of these actors are now giving much thought to how civil societies in the south can be strengthened.

Participation?

Even assuming there were civil society factors capable of dialogue, that does not clarify what participation in the PRSP process is really supposed to mean. In civil society only to be listened to, or can it if necessary refuse to approve a PRSP? What impact would a refusal have on acceptance of the document by the IMF and World Bank and other donor? And in view of the great time pressure, will civil society be at all able to formulate discuss and feed their positions into the process? It could be of decisive importance for the current debate on the PRSP model to delink the urgently needed debt relief from drawing up a PRSP programme, which simply needs more time. For example, it is conceivable that there would be no great problems in granting a country a moratorium on debt servicing so long as a PRSP process is continuing and then for giving debt when it is completed. That would ease the time problem for NGOs and at the same time maintain pressure on governments actually to arrive at poverty reduction strategies that were developed in a participatory process.

Other Causes of Poverty in Developing Countries

The entire current process is focused on the countries of the south, their governments and societies. That diverts attention from the responsibility of the donors and creditors. Not only that the IMF's structural adjustment programmes to date have been counterproductive for fighting poverty (why does the IMF not admit that openly just for once?). Not only that the now promised debt reliefs and coming much too late (the debt crisis of the poorest countries was deplored decades ago!). The present strategy also ignores various other exogenous causes of poverty in the South. What impacts do the finance and trade policies of northern countries have on the modest attempts to enable sustainable development in the South? What consequences will the continuing cutting of development budgets have on the South (no one anyway ventures to talk nowadays about the old 0.7 per cent ODA-GNP ratio)? Fort the donors and creditors to now pass the buck of sole responsibility to the governments of the South and present themselves in the background as noble do-gooders may be a successful strategy in terms of domestic politics, but not an acceptable one for development policy.

14

DEMOCRACY AND POVERTY: ARE THEY INTERLINKED?

Democracy assistance and poverty reduction are rightly becoming two focal—and related—issues for development assistance. Increasingly, many organisations, including intergovernmental, national and civil society, are focusing their work on these two areas. Furthermore, the relationship between these two issues is complex and ever changing. There is thus a need to develop methodologies for linking democracy assistance and poverty reduction at both the policy and programme levels. International IDEA (Institute for Democracy and Electoral Assistance) in cooperation with the World Bank and the United Nations Development Programme, is developing concrete strategies that address these two objectives in a mutually reinforcing way. Through an overall situation analysis followed by regional meetings in sub-Saharan Africa, South Asia, Latin America, the Caucasus and the Arab region, the Institute has marshalled evidence of some of the key problems that affect democracy consolidation and poverty reduction in these countries:

- Corruption and its undermining effect on popular confidence in public institutions;
- Continuing economic instability coupled with the lack of strategies for addressing the twin challenges of poverty and increasing popular participation in its alleviation;

- The extremely limited nature of citizen's influence on overall policy and decision-making processes despite the spread of formal democratic institutions;

- A trend in many post-communist states towards viewing growing poverty as a direct consequence of a transition to democracy.

In short, the evidence is not very encouraging for the prospects for democracy consolidation and poverty reduction. The critical step International IDEA advocates is the development of an approach that not only seeks to put democracy assistance and poverty reduction on top of the devolvement assistance agenda, but also to encourage all involved to treat them as twin elements of an integrated programme of action.

Through a focus on accountable governance, promotion and protection of citizenship and rights and increased popular participation, International IDEA believes that both democracy and poverty reduction can be addressed simultaneously. Policy recommendations are being developed and will be shared in the course of this year with governments, international organisation and civil society bodies.

International IDEA believes that democracy promotion can be used as a tool for fulfilling a variety of objectives. Democracy matters because it protects human rights and preserves human dignity. But democracy also matters because it helps to address some of the most critical challenges facing states today: peace, development, economic growth and stability.

Democracy does not guarantee any one of these, but increasingly it seems to be a precondition for them in the long term. Thus, advocating democracy goes beyond being a moral issue; it becomes *fundamental* to advancing the well-being of people and the stability of states. International IDEA will continue to explore the link between democracy and the major issues facing society today—and continue to argue the case for democracy.

15

CHALLENGING TRADITIONAL ECONOMIC GROWTH

Today, saving the planet is about redefining our economic development models. Striving towards the fulfilment of basic human rights is an integral part of environmental protection. Without a people-centred development strategy we will fail. Conflicting interests and lack of vision and courage are among the many reasons why it is so hard to meet needs in a world of plenty. We are faced with three major challenges in the 1990s.

- To curb population growth and poverty.
- To search for sustainable production and consumption patterns.
- To promote equity.

Population growth is often associated with poverty. But who causes the major strain on the environment? The 1.2 billion poorest people consume small amounts of the world's resources and contribute little to harmful emissions. They do not cause a heavy burden. The day-to-day struggle for survival of the poorest does, however, undermine their resources, and this causes deaths as population grows beyond the carrying capacity of nature. Here two key elements are essential: to turn from non-renewable to renewable resources, and to minimize use of resources through resource efficiency.

We must single out the products and processes and must be phased out and those which may be allowed to expand. Right prices that include the ecological costs will be explored further, together with administrative measures. We are ready to examine the possibilities of using 'green tax' reforms to enhance employment and harness pollution and inefficient resources use. By shifting the burden of taxes from labour to environmentally harmful products and processes we might achieve a double benefit.

Transport, waste management, energy and land use and obvious areas that need to be affected by policy changes. Individuals must use their power as green-conscious citizens and shoppers—but, in the end, producers and service providers hold the main key to practical action.

The market must be harnessed to meet people's needs both for present and future generations—starting by making economic policies play by the rules of nature. The World Trade Organisation (WTO) negotiations have provided us with instruments to regulate world trade.

Getting the Prices Right

Car emissions may be cut drastically, but the rapid increase of new cars nullifies the benefits. Even the most ardent technological optimist must admit that we need new priorities or cuts in some products and services. For example, we must improve public transport and resource-efficient cars—and reduce traffic.

Traditional economic growth models fall short of solving the problem of unemployment. Indeed, 'roobots' and wasteful resource use replace people. There are great job-creating possibilities in environment-friendly produces and processes. Striving towards equity within and between nations, and within and between generations, is the major challenge of our time.

The fact that 20 per cent of the world's population consumes 80 per cent of the world's resources has too long been seen as mainly an ethical challenge. Ethics are not easily translated into politics, especially when confronted with economic and market realities. As equity gradually becomes a security issue—as it will, if we do not bridge the gaps within and between nations—it will climb to the top of the political agenda.

Many of the main conflict areas of today are battlefields of resource management. These will expand greatly if we do not turn conference statements of good intention into action. The 30-year old commitment of the rich countries to meet the target of 0.7 per cent of GNP in official Development Assistance remains unmet.

Two hundred years of Western-led development optimism reached its peak in the late 1980s. When the Berlin wall fell, the economic growth models of the rich countries had become the universal recipe. But as more and more people aspire to join the ranks of the middle classes, the resulting environmental stress calls for a halt, or a radical change of course.

The call for new patterns of production and consumption challenges our traditional concepts of economic growth and the focus on materialism in our culture. Neither the industrialised nor the poorer countries are strangers to radical process of change, through the reasons for change are shifting. And we are truly facing challenging and conflict-provoking changes.

No nation by itself can solve the problems we face. Pollution knows no frontiers, but comes to us with the winds and waves. We have become more and more interdependent. If we are to attain sustainable development, we must commit ourselves through international agreements, through an international rule of law, through the development of financial mechanisms and through institutional agreements. We must develop means and tools to enhance collective security and mutual interests.

16

TECHNOLOGICAL ENTREPRENEURSHIP: THE NEW FORCE FOR ECONOMIC GROWTH

Entrepreneurship has emerged as a major new force for change. The dynamic role of modern small business in economic growth has received fresh recognition worldwide. It is essential to promote entrepreneurship and to mobilise the dynamism of the private sector for accelerated national development. An unbridled private sector may not, however, ensure growth with equity. It is the prime responsibility of governments to create policy frameworks that enable businesses to apply technology for competitive advantage and for the well-being of the public.

The Changing Global Environment

As agents of change and progress, entrepreneurs start by identifying a market opportunity and matching this with social or technical innovations. They them proceed to mobilise the resources necessary to drive their business concept to its commercial realisation. The development of a product or service with a high-technology content-never easy anywhere, or at today's rapidly-changing global environment. It calls for restructuring the available technology and business development systems and developing the skills needed by a new breed of "techno-entrepreneurs" to transform innovations into market opportunities at home and abroad. It also requires reorienting the present processes and priorities of technical and economic cooperation among countries.

Amidst the global concerns of environmental preservation, poverty elimination and social development, the practical problems of entrepreneurship are not being properly addressed, even though entrepreneurs will create the bulk of enterprises, jobs and wealth.

A torrent of technology-based goods hits the market every week, ostensibly improving the quality of our lives while simultaneously creating complexity and dislocation. The pace of progress in information technologies, microelectronics, robotics, new materials, biomedical sciences, space science and other advanced technologies quickens, significantly changing the way we live. The growth of markets for these technologies also proceeds apace.

Further, technological change is taking place today against a background of growing intra-national and international disequilibria. While the transformation from State-centred to market-oriented development is opening up enormous opportunities and options, it has also caused severe short-terms hardships. In order to survive and prosper in these changing times, India and its enterprises need enlightened government policies, good technical infrastructure and strong cultural roots.

Traditional production factors are giving way to a new paradigm characterised by new patterns of trade, investment and employment, and by informal networking life-long learning and technological entrepreneurship. The manufacturing sector in India continues to be dominated by food products, textiles, chemicals and other traditional industry, mainly in the public sector. However, change is coming, albeit slowly. State enterprises are being corporatised pending privatisation, and the share of knowledge-based and information-related activities in the marketplace is rising perceptibly. Restructuring policies now place emphasis (often purely rhetorical) on the role of the private sector. The legacy of decades of centrally-planned development is generally inimical to private enterprise. In turn, the private sector has been slow to respond to economic liberalisation in India and generally failed to generate the new employment necessary to absorb new entrants to the labour force.

The regulatory problems of an onerous tax structure and administration, poor access to finance and raw materials, over-regulation of labour and land use, pervasive bureaucracy and restricted markets have been significant barriers to entrepreneurial growth.

Towards Competitive Performance

The imperative of improved performance has serious implications for India if it is to survive, stay abreast and succeed. It calls from national efforts on systemic efficiency and productivity growth, the move from an investment-driven to an innovation-driven economy and sustained higher-order competitiveness; towards enhanced customer satisfaction at home and penetration of selected markets abroad. Concurrently, governments and business have to address such intractable problems as poverty, corruption and the degradation of the environment.

Creating New Technology-based Ventures

Starting a new business in India is a hazardous task. Problems are compounded when the venture is technology-based:

- Capital requirements are generally larger, while traditional banks are ill-equipped to process the perceived risk. Venture capital generally only becomes an option when the venture has documented the merits of its management, market and innovation.
- Knowledge-based ventures can benefit from linkages to sources of knowledge—e.g. the technical university or research lab. Such mentoring needs to be cultivated.

- Techno-entrepreneurs often have technical skills but usually lack the business management and marketing skills necessary for success. These need to be supplemented.

- In fields where technology is changing rapidly, it is often advantageous to make technology-acquisition arrangements. Sourcing such innovations, negotiating technology licensing agreements and protecting the intellectual property itself require special skills.

- Knowledge-based innovations are inherently more risky than others. The management of this unique risk requires assessment techniques and vision.

- Technology-based ventures often have social and environmental implications, which need to be managed carefully.

- Penetrating a competitive market requires good market intelligence, a good strategic plan and good luck.

Special Characteristics of 'Techno-entrepreneurs'

The popular misconceptions are that techno-entrepreneurs are born, not made; that they take risks with other people's money and fail more often than they succeeded. In fact, entrepreneur skills can be identified and developed. The entrepreneur is typically an innovator who formulates new solutions to existing problems, mobilizes resources and stimulates others to participate in his or her team. These aptitudes develop over time, often starting in childhood, as the person faces new challenges and learns from failure.

Entrepreneurial opportunities can be found in every industrialising country, community and family. Principal sources of entrepreneurs for knowledge-based ventures are often the university and government research laboratories, the large industrial and military establishments and professional service firms. Some motivations of the entrepreneur are the need to: be independent; create value; contribute to society; earn recognition; become rich or; quite often, simply not to be employed. Value-adding ventures with good growth potential can best be developed in an open market and in a culture which supports risk-taking.

The techno-entrepreneur anywhere has the challenge of moving a concept through the prototype and production phases towards creation of a product which meets market needs at a price consistent with the value created and with the ability of customers to pay.

Equally important, the market itself has to be developed and sustained. It is not enough to be first with a better mousetrap if one does not have the skills to educate and reach potential buyers and to set the market standard.

Hence one has to distinguish between innovators and inventors. The inventor is typically a creative person in a quest for knowledge or for producing new products, without determining in advance whether a real market exists for his or her inventions. On the other hand, the innovator draws on existing knowledge and the talents of others to develop or adapt a product or service at a volume and cost that can capture a significant portion of an identified market. The flexibility and creativity of a small entrepreneurial techno-venture may lead to more incremental and break-through innovations that can be generated by larger-sized firms in many sectors.

The pace and pattern of India's economic development now depend in large measure on its technical resource base. In this context, the key determinants are the skills to apply technology for enhanced competitiveness, as well as to create techbased ventures. Techno-entrepreneurs have to be supported by appropriate national structures and international linkages if they are to survive and flourish in an intensely competitive world.

17

DEVELOPMENT: THE PEOPLE KNOW BEST

Meetings of the World Bank and the World Trade Organisation has inspired high-mined protest and, on occasion, even vandalism. But this protest and vandalism may miss the point. It is hard to blame those who complain of bullying or blundering by the great institutions of global power. But the poor of the world, especially the poor of developing countries, deserve more than street demonstrations. The poor understand better than anybody the complicated details of their own poverty—the absence of health care, the lack of education, and all the minister perils to their own safety and well-being. They know the failures of their governments, and of international institutions.

And that is the point: it is the people of the poor countries who will have to apply new knowledge to design and achieve their own development. A country can only develop when its citizens have the freedom to address their own development problems. The obligation of the rich countries, is to give help where they can. And anyone who doesn't see a moral imperative to contribute to a fairer, more prosperous future is free to frame the obligation differently—as self-interest, for example. It will surely serve us better to invest in a peaceful and contended global community than to invite the strife and poverty of unanswered injustice and economic ruin.

Among our relevant conclusions: Powerful institutions of global finance and trade (not least, the World Bank and the

World Trade Organisation) can be a source of real promise to poor countries. If governed right, they can help integrate developing economies into the enriching opportunities of global trade and investment. But such promise is often wasted because the very poverty of poor-country governments weakens their ability to negotiate the terms that would serve them best.

Communities in poor countries find themselves at a special disadvantage when it comes to bargaining with foreign investors. Investment can bring growth and spread wealth. It can also threaten human rights and social cohesion, or cultural integrity, and the fragile balance of ecosystems. Noble economist Amartyasen has spoken powerfully about the intimate relation between development and choice, the subject of his thought-provoking book Development as Freedom. Development, Sen argues, "consists of the removal of various types of unfreedoms that leave people with little choice and little opportunity..." He defines freedom as "both the primary end and the principal means of development."

A precondition of this freedom is knowledge—knowledge of the hard facts and the hard science, on which real choices are constructed, Also it is knowledge of good governance—procedures of choice that are effective, responsive and democratic. For budgetary reasons, rich countries contribution to international development was severely cut in the 1990s. Now, along with others in the rich countries, they have to begin to reinvest in international development.

This means a new commitment to the improvement of lives, and to the future that the North must share with the South. It will be a reinvestment in peace, and in our own prosperity. This remains a matter of obligation, and of sensible self-interest.

18

CAN ECONOMIC GROWTH REDUCE POVERTY?

New Findings on Inequality, Economic Growth and Poverty

Many people still think first of 'economic growth' in relation to poverty reduction. Indeed, their correlation is one of the most-discussed issues of combating poverty. The relationship is of great importance because if there is a clear causal dependency, reducing poverty could fundamentally be limited to measures to promote growth. However, if there was low growth or stagnation it would not be possible to reduce poverty decisively. In the opposite case, that of the phenomena having no causal relation, promising measures to reduce poverty could be taken up even without economic growth.

Hardly anyone now explicitly expresses the view that economic development trickles down automatically to the poor. Practical experience has refuted this assumption dating from the early days of development policy in the 1960s. However, a number of studies show development of growth and a decline in poverty running parallel. On the other hand, there are also examples which show that despite high economic growth, poverty is not reduced markedly. The common answer to the question this raises is thus: Yes, growth can reduce poverty, but only if additional measures oriented on the poor are taken up. This is often termed pro-poor-growth. But what that means in detail, and whether economic growth as such plays a causal role at all, is not clarified. It is worth taking a look at the arguments on the basis of more recent empirical and theoretical knowledge.

No Direct Causality Between Growth and Poverty Reduction

Among the many indicators of poverty, the income of the poor (income poverty) has the closest relationship to economic growth. An increase in gross domestic product and thus national income could, if other factors come into play be linked with an increase in the per capita income of the poor.

Such a relationship between economic growth and the income of the poor, however, cannot be described as causal, as is asserted implicitly time and again by the statement that growth is a necessary but not sufficient precondition for poverty reduction. In so far as growth and poverty reduction arise at the same time at the end of a process, they exist alongside each other. It would be almost a tautology to say that the former is the cause or part-cause of the latter. Both express the samething, namely a change in per capita income as well, and both have similar causes. What matters is recognising what these causes are and what specific factors must come into play so that the income of the poor grows too. Growth as a "prerequisite" or "condition" is then no longer the focus; the priority is asking for specific policies that result in higher incomes for the poor. The detour in thinking about growth is not necessary. Since, however, it is based on similar factors, such as fiscal policy/budget structure, employment policy, combating inflation, and institutional development, economic growth can also emerge if poverty is reduced. The difference of views lies in the fact that under the heading 'poverty reduction' the aim is no longer growth, but a purposeful reduction of poverty.

Therefore, in reverse, successful combating of poverty can be seen as being the cause of growth insofar as activating the capabilities of the poor and using their productive capacity of the poor and using their productive capacity triggers economic drive.

Indirect Causality Between Growth and Poverty Reduction?

So even if economic growth fundamentally has no direct causal impact on poverty, growth still can reduce it indirectly. This is the case when due to positive economic development a government has greater revenue and uses the surplus for combating poverty, for example by providing such public goods as education and health services. Also in these cases, however, growth is not a compelling precondition. Even without growth greater government revenue can be achieved for example by more efficient tax collection. And leeway for social welfare spending can be gained by redistributing the budget, such as by cutting military appropriations. Furthermore, an automatic process is not given because the government can also use surplus funds for non-social purposes.

Creation of jobs due to increased economic activity can be another indirect link between economic growth and income poverty, if such a development generates income and reduces poverty. But also in this case I see no compelling causality because, for instance, industrial jobs are not necessarily open to the really poor. In addition, these positive impacts occur to a considerable extent only in the event of labour-intensive development. In many countries, however, economic growth is achieved by capital-intensive production.

Inequality, Growth and Income Poverty

If national incomes, grow, a naive observer might assume that the income of the poor must also grow along with it. But that would be a statistical fallacy. Even if only the income of the rich grows, this results in macro-economic statistics showing a higher per capita income. What the true conditions are, is shown as soon as one divides the population statistically into income groups, such as in fifths, as is usual. It then turns out that the bald figures on average per capita growth can certainly cloak a situation where the income of the richest fifth of the population is growing fast while that of the poorest fifth is stagnating. Despite growth, the gap between the two becomes even wider.

The unequal distribution of income (and of other assets such as property and access to social services), and its connection to poverty reduction and growth as recently returned to the forefront of the debate.

It is obvious that inequality and its changes have direct effects on the poverty situation. Does inequality also have an impact on poverty via its relation to growth, because growth promotes or reduces inequality? Earlier, the predominant view was that rapid growth was linked with atleast a temporary increase in inequality, so that a distinct policy of growth initially disadvantaged the poor.

The current dominant view is that growth has no foreseeable effects on inequality and that inequality changes only very slowly, in reverse, however, it is assumed that greater equality is a determinant of growth. According to that view, an indirect relationship between poverty on one side and inequality as a factor dependent upon growth on the other is not given.

That leads to the conclusion that fair distribution has more weight than growth. Fair distribution, however does not depend upon growth. An appropriate policy is possible at any time, not only after an economic situation has improved. The notion that still shimmers through the debate that "something must be earned first before it can be distributed", is wrong. It is a matter of designing policy and the entire economic process right from the start in such a way that the surplus benefits all including the poor. Important elements of such a policy are, for examples, land reform and development of finance systems.

Relationship of Growth to Poverty

According to today's conventional wisdom, income poverty expresses only a part of what poverty means. Not least through the voices of the poor themselves, it has become clear that violation of human dignity and rights, a lack of participation in decisions and exclusion from society, unequal treatment of men and women and vulnerability are also regarded as poverty. For poverty is caused to a great degree by conflicts of power and interests. Income poverty often is not even seen the greatest problem.

What relationship do these more far reaching characteristics of poverty have to economic growth? A direct relationship of growth to socially-related aspects such as women's inheritance rights, land rights and exclusion from decisions cannot been seen. Considerable improvements in favour of the poor can be achieved here even without economic growth.

Those who see a strong and causal connection between economic growth and poverty reduction must ask themselves what the prospects are for high growth and poverty reduction must ask themselves what the prospects are for high growth rates and thus for a decline in poverty. Coupling poverty reduction to economic growth is problematic. If only low growth rates are to be expected.

Another question is whether continuous increase in growth are at all desirable and possible in the medium to long term. In this connection, a difference should perhaps be made between developing countries and industrialised nations. But environmental compatibility and availability of resources set limits to growth for both. Some academics assume that industrialised nations have already reached an inherent limit (stagnation theory) and that the high growth rates of earlier years will not return. Moreover, they add, full employment is no longer achievable due to, among other things, an ongoing increase in productivity, and current unemployment cannot be reduced by customary means. In any case, if growth were to be taken as the major benchmark, the prospects for a radical reduction of income poverty around the world would be modest.

Summing Up

Poverty is a complex problem and reducing it depends upon many interconnected factors that is why poverty cannot be attributed to one main cause nor its reduction based on one main strategy. Economic growth is just one strategic element among many others related to poverty reduction. An indirect causal connection between growth and poverty reduction can only be seen because governments will have a greater scope for action due to economic growth, and if they promote labour-intensive development.

Therefore growth's role in poverty reduction must be put into perspective. Growth cannot be the first thing that comes to mind, nor is it the golden path to reducing poverty. The simplistic theory of economic growth as the main condition obstructs the bigger picture; it clings to the underlying and ongoing belief in the trickle-down effect. Even if there is no growth or for inherent reasons there can he none, there are promising ways to take on the challenge of mass poverty in the developing countries. Up front, governments and bilateral and multilateral donors must have the political will to design economic, financial and social policies so that they are oriented on poverty in a coherent way—the result can also be economic growth.

19

BEYOND ECONOMICS

Unless policymakers take a more all-round view of education, they risk sending their countries down the wrong path. Over the past decade, educational change in most countries has been driven by one imperative: survival in the global economy. This process has been particularly salient in the Asia-Pacific region following the drastic shock of the 1997 economic downturn. But in the current reform process, marked by speeding commercialisation and economic preoccupations, other educational missions are being ignored, and countries risk paying a high price for their short-sightedness.

There's no denying that economic considerations are critical in today's world. Students have to acquire the knowledge and skills to survive and compete in the global economy, especially one which more than ever before prizes human capital. A high-quality labour force gives nations a cutting edge in global competition. Understandably, stressing economic returns in the current educational debate attracts private resources. But education has other functions that are the indispensable corollary of more balanced, equitable development. They deserve to be briefly explained.

The first is a social function: education has role to play in facilitating social mobility and bringing about integration in often very diverse constituencies. It is at school that children learn how to form a broader set of relationships, to live together and become aware of belonging to teach us civic attitudes, to make us aware of our rights and responsibilities—in essence, to become responsible citizens. The task is fundamental in light of democracy's advance in so many countries over the past decade or so. Then there is education's cultural function. Developing creativity and aesthetic awareness, accepting other traditions and belief systems while valuing our own are all part of the path towards fulfilment. Finally, education is a goal in and of itself. Schools help children learn how to learn and play a pivotal role in transferring knowledge from one generation to the next. I believe that all these facets of learning are critical for the long-term prosperity of our societies. In our globalised, interdependent world, these functions take on a more international character. Everywhere, education has a role to play in eliminating racial and gender biases. Promoting global common interests, moments for peace, and greater international understanding.

Rising above Short-term Pressures to Strike a Harmonious Balance

While education is widely recognised as the spine of the learning society, the complexity lies in striking a balance between these various functions. The commercialisation of education that we are witnessing the world over inevitably pushes schools, educators, parents and policymakers to pursue short-term, market-driven outcomes. Lawyers, bankers and businessmen have an increasingly high profile in educational debate. Following Southeast Asia's downturn in 1997, they were influential in changing the academic mindset. In little time, emphasis has shifted from academic achievement to developing communication skills, creativity, adaptability. In and of itself, this is not necessarily regrettable. The problem is that these skills are all perceived to be at the service of a supreme economic value.

Sounder research will be required to analyse and assess where the current trends are leading us. It is increasingly recognized, however, that unless economic growth is accompanied by good governance, a fair sharing of benefits, better social and environmental protection and attention to culture, it will, sooner or later, lead to unrest. It is through education that this broad spectrum of concerns can be nurtured. Policymakers who have taken stock of this holistic mission unfortunately represent a minority in today's educational debates and reforms. Their foremost challenge is to manage commercialization, to rise above short-term pressures and to take a more ethical stance towards education, a long-term strategic view.

20

UNEMPLOYMENT IN THE POOR AND RICH WORLDS

Different Causes, but Converging Policies?

In view of the magnitude of global unemployment, all the customary formulas offered by economists against mass unemployment—the basic socio-economic problem of modern times—appear to be quackery. Neither quantitative, nor any kin of 'qualitative', growth will be able to eliminate the disastrous worldwide lack of jobs. For ecological reasons it is impossible to include 800 million or more unemployed in the production process through corresponding growth. The resulting increase in global Gross Domestic Product would require consumption of natural resources, energy and the environment which, given even the greatest possible productivity in those sectors, could not even be sustained for two or three decades.

In addition, aiming to achieve full employment through growth will be ever more difficult even in the rich economies. For it is most likely that work productivity will continue to rise worldwide. Countries such as China, which are in the initial phase of modernisation, are still producing at a relatively still low productivity rate. But that is precisely why they can achieve notable increases in productivity in a short time by importing technology from highly-developed countries. The advantage of rapid 'catch-up rationalisation', however, is being bought at the cost of rising unemployment and progressive impoverishment.

Employment Through Redistribution of Work

The notion that jobs can at some time be created for 800-900 million unemployed who will work 35 or even 40 hours a week at the productivity level of the highly-developed countries of four or five decades ago is absurd. The only realistic possibility of eliminating the world's unemployment problem is by far-reaching redistribution of work and income. The change needed for that demands fundamentally new concepts of prosperity: a reflection on the philosophy of the 'life of happiness'. 'New concepts of prosperity' means that technological progress would no longer be used mainly to deliver rising per capita incomes and excessive consumption. Instead, given a sufficient material standard of living, the quality of life would be improved primarily by shortening working hours. It is about, so to speak, assigning socio-instrumental good sense new goals. Plus reshaping socio-economic conditions in such a way that the politicians will again be compelled to orient themselves on the good of the community and humanistic values instead of filling the pockets of the wealthy. It is sheer ideology, although very persuasive, to cite 'globalisation' and its alleged 'iron laws' in defaming the welfare state, full employment and social justice as out-of-date wishful thinking. A return to the state-guided social competitive system as practised during the first decades after the Second World War is possible just as it was politically feasible to make the transition from the old order of unfettered, ruthless capitalism to the mixed economies of the social market economy types. So it is a matter of restoring the proven structures of a mixed economic system.

However, in contrast of the first postwar decades it is now not sufficient to regenerate nation-state interventionism. Appropriate international regulations are required. Above all, it will depend upon reversing the new laissez-faire developments in international economic relationships which today are subsumed under the buzzword 'globalisation'. That is, to oppose over-liberalisation and its disastrous social and inhuman impacts. It will depend on the broad mobilisation of the losers in the process of globalisation whether the necessary fundamental change of course can still be made in time before a catastrophe. In particular, the new myth must be opposed that declares globalisation as a kind of nature and thus suggests resignation and adaptation to an allegedly unavoidable process of destruction of social and human achievements.

Mass Unemployment in the Poor Economies

The employment problems in the rich and the poor hemispheres differ not only in their magnitude, but also in their causes. The wretched condition of the poor economies is due above all to historical reasons: colonialism and, in the post-colonial era, the constraints to independent development imposed by the hegemonic influence of the rich industrial states. The waste of scarce resources by international and civil wars, and the dictatorships with their upperclass luxury consumption and inefficient, thus development-obstructing exploitation structures—often supported by the industrialised nations—have for a long time repressed and in many cases destroyed autonomous development potential. The colonial and post-colonial distortion also contributed at least indirectly to the current population problems of the poor countries. The politically inflicted mass poverty and under-development stabilised or in fact brought about economic, socio-psychological and ideological mechanisms which oppose an effective population policy. As we know, the average educational level in many developing countries, especially among women, is too low to give a modern population policy a chance of success. Mass unemployment in the poor countries is the result of poverty. In this respect, it is about a production-side problem: too few resources, too little real and human capital, and the inefficient, unproductive use of much of the anyway limited added value of society. The picture is totally different in the rich countries—the over-production economies.

Unemployment in Over-production Systems

The main cause of mass unemployment in the industrialised nations has nothing to do with shortages. It is a phenomenon of surplus. Greater possibilities of production can no longer be used 'sufficiently' profitably because the required demand is lacking. Production is done for profit. The necessary collateral condition is the satisfying of consumer needs. Employment is not even such a conditions, but only a side effect which lapses immediately when labour-free production is technically possible. Thus, national income must be shared among wages and profits (or income from property). Profit is the difference between earnings and costs. Earnings depend upon demand. Macro-economic costs consist mainly of wages and salaries (including social security contributions). These definitive connections mean that profit can be made only if overall demand is greater than the total cost of labour. But in the final analysis this demand can only come from the profit-earners themselves. In his book, a Treatise on Money, Keynes described this nexus as the theory of the Widow's cruse. Under capitalistic conditions, labour is only sought or hired if profit can be earned with it. But as making a profit depends upon the demand for consumption and investment by the shareholders, it can be seen that the degree of employment is determined by the demand behaviour of the class that receives income from property. In this respect, the widespread belief that greater investment also leads to more employment, namely via the effect of investment in demand, is right.

Lower Wages Mean Lower Demand

The lower the level of wages, and given an unchanged total demand, the greater are the profits that can be made. But it is more likely that in the case of falling wages the overall demand will also drop. For stabilising total demand would require the recipients of income from property to increase their spending on consumption and/or investment to the degree to which wages and the consumption based on them fell.

During the last 10 to 15 years the development of profits in most industrialised nations has been very favourable. But profits would have grown more strongly if the demand of the shareholders had been much greater. This would have created more employment at the same time. Thus, it can be assumed that the profits are simply too high for the shareholders to be able to go in for meaningful consumption or make profitable investments. That is the reason for the extreme redirection of capital from fixed assets to portfolio investment. The growth of speculative (unproductive) financial transactions during the 1980s and 1990s (buzzword: casino capitalism), corresponded with a relatively weak formation of real capital.

Wage rises, of course, narrow the scope for profit. But precisely this effect stimulated efforts to improve the profit situation not only by investment in rationalisation, but also by investment in expansion aimed at the growing mass purchasing power. Since more is being invested, the profit mass also is growing according to the principle of the Widow's cruse. Too low wages, as it were, relieve the shareholders of the pressure to innovate and invest and allow them to earn their profits too easily. That is the real message of the 'purchasing power theory' of wages.

Over-accumulation and Under-consumption

Overproduction has two different causes which, however, mostly occur in tandem. They are over-investment, or creation of over-capacities, on the one hand, and lack of demand due to relative saturation and an absence of mass purchasing power on the other. But the main reason for mass unemployment in the rich hemisphere currently lies on the demand side. During the first three decades after the Second World War supply and demand rose in relative balance. Economic fluctuations showed up as temporary declines in generally positive GDP growth rates. These decades of (dynamic) balance of growth are often described today as the era of 'Fordism'. Its essential feature is that rising wages ensure continuing growth of consumption, so that equally growing profits also flow relatively continuously into investments to expand capacity and create jobs. The label 'Fordism' expresses the 'simple' view of the theory of the buying power of wages which is said to have been propagated by Henry Ford I. This was that his workers should earn enough to be able to buy the cars they made.

The astonishingly balanced development of supply and demand from 1950 to the mid-1970s was due above all to postwar reconstruction and the pent-up demand of consumers who were starved by wartime economy shortages. This stimulated positive investment sentiment, and high investments brought at the same time high profits. The postwar growth that led within a short time to full employment was also linked with growth in productivity which on multi-year average was more than twice that of the crisis period of the last 25 years. Thus, the so-called employment threshold (the GDP growth rate point at which employment growth begins) was much higher in those days than it is now, although there was full employment over a longer period. This simple fact opposes the thesis often propounded today that mass unemployment is above all related to rationalisation. It is not rationalisation per se, that is, progress that boosts productivity, which is the evil. The problem is that the mistakes in distribution policy which are rooted in capitalistic structures result in increases in supply encountering insufficient demand for goods, whereby the demand for labour drops. However, the fact that demand policy contradicts the requirements of a social ethic that is ecologically responsible and right for the interests of the poor countries was already spelled out. So if a demand-oriented growth policy is practised at all, it should be designed to be as environmentally compatible as possible. After all, there are possibilities for that, such as by expanding the production of services that spare resources. A one hour driving lesson costs more energy than one hour of ballet instruction.

The politically initiated and implemented over-liberalisation and surrender of social prosperity to global competition since the 1970s, which reproduces that old self-destructive mechanism of laissez faire, have during the last two decades markedly accelerated the crisis development inherent in the system.

Summing up, It is Noted That:

- full employment in the rich economies would certainly be possible by means of demand policy, but only at a high cost to the environment that is concomitant with high growth rates;
- the growth policy of the rich countries impairs the poor conomies' possibilities of medium to long-term growth, since these are falling back ever further in the competition for ever scarcer and thus ever more expensive resources;
- the environmental collapse currently expected for the third or fourth generation after us, which obviously also will trigger a collapse of the world economy and—probably ahead of that—armed conflicts which today are hardly imaginable, would happen very much sooner if economic growth were to be increased to such a degree that it would bring full employment worldwide;
- in the long term, the problem of global unemployment and global poverty can only be solved by a policy of massive redistribution, and in fact a redistribution of work and income, whereby increases in productivity must be used mainly or only for shortening working hours. That is a demand which appears to be utopians. But utopias of today often have the quality of scripting the reality of tomorrow.

21

CONSUMING THE FUTURE

Now that we are to reach six billion of us, it is a good point to check again on what sort of lifestyles we pursue and what is the environmental impact of those lifestyles. It is curious that we have spent several decades being concerned about the growing numbers of humankind while not giving at least an equal amount of attention to the levels of living we aspire to, and how many natural resources we chew up thereby and how much pollution and waste we cause.

Everybody is a consumer of sorts. True, every fifth person scarcely qualifies for that designation, consuming goods worth less than $1 per day. Conversely, every seventh person qualifies for a designation of super-consumer, with a cash income at least fifty times greater. These latter are the people who, through their carbon dioxide emissions, are disrupting everybody's climate dozens of times more than the average citizen of one Earth. Fair play, anyone?

Much as the have-nots seek to match the haves, it is plain their efforts will not work out for a long time to come, at best. If every Chinese person were to consume just one additional chicken per year and if the said chicken were to be raised primarily on grain, this would account for as much grain per year as all the grain exports of the number two exporter, Canada. If the Chinese were to raise their per-capita consumption of beef, now only 4 kgs per year, to that of Americans, 45 kg, and if the additional beef were produced largely in feedlots after the manner of the United States, it would account for as much extra grain as the entire US grain harvest, less than one-third of which is exported. Because of its recent climbing up the food chain toward a meet-based diet, China has become one of the world's leading importers of grain. The global grain market today is around 200 million tones per year, and shows scant scope for significant increase.

As a further measure of its ambitions, the Chinese government has designated the auto industry as one of five industry "pillars". Today China has fewer cars than Los Angeles. If per-capita car ownership, together will oil consumption, were to match that of the United States, China would need 80 million barrels of oil per day—by contrast with the world's 1996 oil output of 64 million barrels of oil per day. The surge in carbon dioxide emissions would be unprecedented.

All this notwithstanding, there are already some 250 million newly affluent people in China. They are people with a household income equivalent to perhaps US$ 20,000, and enough discretionary income to enjoy the perquisites of the good life as perceived by these nouveaux riches. Top of the shopping lists are meat and more meat, followed by cars whether big or small. These are the badges of success: they show you have Arrived.

The new consumers in China are matched by at least 200 million in India, and tens of millions in South Korea, Taiwan, Malaysia and Thailand (the recent economic setbacks have not permanently punctured the economic bubbles). Then there are 200 million more in Brazil, Argentina, Venezuela and Mexico, and more again in Hungary and other countries of Eastern Europe, also Turkey. Put them all together and they total about as many as the 800 million long established consumers in the ultra rich countries (the OECD grouping). When the current economic hiccups in Asia are left behind, the ranks of the new consumers can be expected to rise rapidly.

But they cannot hope to become super consumers. Where would all the extra gain come from? How could the global climate tolerate the huge additional pulse of carbon dioxide? There are all kinds of other environmental reasons to suppose that environmental constraints will become all the more constraining. True, technology could help moderate the environmental impact. We could enjoy twice as much material prosperity while using only half as much natural resources and causing half as much pollution and waste. But the new consumers will want to pursue the American dream to the hilt, and it is hard to see that the best technologies could enable huge numbers of affluent aspirants, perhaps two billion people by 2010, enjoying even half the material prosperity of Americans with average household incomes of $ 40,000.

But is it true 'prosperity'—mental and emotional as well as material? Or is the American dream becoming a nightmare with its harried lifestyles and declining leisure time, where the shopping mall is the ultimate mecca, and the good life is a case of piling up goodies?

In any case, we cannot expect the new consumers to forgo their 'rightful share' of affluence unless the longtime affluent agree to cut back on their environmental ruinous lifestyles. It is these communities that must offer a strong example, and soonest. Where is the political leader who will espouse the new vision, however much it may be perceived as the ultimate vote loser?

22

CONSUMPTION BOMB

It is three decades since we passed the peak world population growth rate of 2.04 per cent. Annual additions too are now a decade past their peak of 86 Million a year. They are currently running at 78 Million a year and are heading downwards. A peak in total numbers, however, still lies at least four or five decades ahead. On the UN Population Division's 1998 projections, the total is likely to reach 8.9 billion in 2050. The long range medium projection, which has not been updated since 1996, expects world population to level out a just under 11 billion in 2200 AD.

However, this is based on assumptions that are increasingly questionable. More and more countries are reaching levels of female fertility that are not enough for replacement—below 2.1 children over the life time of each women. At the latest count there are 61 countries in this category. Of this 23 had very low fertility, below 1.5.

This situation is unprecedented in times of global peace on economic growth. The UN medium projection assumes that were fertility is very low it will rise again to 1.7-1.9 children per woman. In all countries where fertility is currently above replacement level of 2.1, it assumes that it will not fall below that level.

Yet fertility has fallen below replacement level in so many countries, which such different cultures and different stages of economic growth, that is increasingly looking as if low fertility may be here to stay. If this became the case, then world population may peak at some where between 8 and 9 billion. There after it may well begin to decline. The 1996 long range low projection has world population falling to 5.6 billion in 2100 AD.

None of this means that reproductive rights should have lower priority in future. Their contribution to the health and welfare of women and children and clear. Many poor countries in Africa and South Asia face huge population increases which will be hard to accommodate without major problems of land and water scarcity. In these areas reproductive rights receive a very high priority.

Increasingly our concern must focus on consumption, and how we can cope with the effects of its inexorable increase. Over the past 25 years, world population increased by 53 per cent, but world consumption per person (Measured by income) by only 39 per cent. Assume that consumption per person will rise 100 per cent, while population will rise by only half that amount. As time goes on the preponderance of consumption will increase more and more.

There is a crucial difference between population and consumption aspirations. If fully assured of children's survival most people have quite modest desires for family size. But their desire to consume knows no upper bounds. As wealth increases, people double-up their possessions; two or three cars, two bathrooms, two rooms with all contents, two or three holidays a year.

Appliances improve every year and old ones "need" replacing. New needs are created that never existed before. Globalisation is making products cheaper than ever. TVs are no longer uncommon even in African shanty towns. The number of households is increasing as people live longer and family breakdown becomes more common. Smaller households consume considerably more per cent than large. Moreover, consumption is politically very difficult to restrain.

No-one can get elected promising people they can earn and spend less, or re-elected if they fulfil their promises.

In view of this much of the burden of reducing our environmental impact will rest on technology. Technology will have to deliver major shifts in improving resource productivity, and in reducing the amount of waste we create. All our institutions and forms of management which affect technology will need to be geared to this end.

In some areas the record has been good and looks likely to remain so. Productivity has kept up with demand in the case of resources that are traded on markets, and that are under the direct control of people or companies affected by shortages or prices. Global food production has kept pace with demand: although land and cereal production per person has declined, average intakes of calories and protein have continued to improve and are at record levels. Malnutrition persists, but this is due to poverty and landlessness, not to the inability of the world to produce enough food. We have not encountered any limiting shortage of any key mineral resources or of energy. Nor are we likely to, because we continually economise and find substitutes, there has been a gradual reduction in the material used for each unit of production.

The prospects are much worse for resources that are not traded on markets or subject to sustainable management, as yet. These include groundwater, state forests, ocean fish, biodiversity in general. They include communal waste sinks life rivers, lakes and oceans, and the global atmosphere. In all of these areas it looks likely that things will get quite a lot worse before they get better.

These kinds of resources and sinks are not under the direct control of people affected by shortage or damage. People wishing to change the way a common resource or sink is used or managed have to pass through the legal or political system. They must organise, take out lawsuits against polluters, pressurise legislators and so on. Political responses are typically slow. Usually the majority of voters have to be convinced of the need for action before politicians will risk taking action. Even then powerful and rich vested interests will lobby hard for the status quo, and will often succeed in frustrating changes that are desired by a global majority. America's coal, oil, and car lobbies have stood in the way of any significant US commitment to reduce carbon dioxide output, and the US is the world's largest emitter of carbon dioxide.

Usually there has to be very wide spread and very visible environmental damage before action is taken. The thinning of the ozone layer fitted that category well and the response was swift. North Atlantic fishing reached that point in the 1990s, yet politicians shied away from taking adequate action until the last moment: fishing stocks plummeted and there was massive job loss. Global warming is still long way from the damage being widespread enough, and attributable clearly enough to human activities, for politicians to be ready to speed up the move into renewable energy.

The question with the common resources and sinks is always: will we react in time? The answer is all the more difficult because we usually don't know in advance what is 'in time'. Many critical changes are subject to threshold effects. When a certain point is crossed, very sudden and disastrous change can occur with little warning. In many cases we do not know where the thresholds lie.

Prudence dictates a preventive approach—a stitch in time saves nine. But the history of environmental problems shows that politicians rarely act decisively until the brink is reached, and it will always be touch and go whether we are pushed over it or not.

23

SOCIAL DEVELOPMENT: THE WAY FORWARD

The idea of development is seductive; it is also elusive. It promises a lot to everyone, but it has failed to deliver to those in greatest need. In 1944 development and economic growth were largely synonymous, but by the 1950s, when it became clear that this model was not helping the poor, a focus on social development evolved. Its advocates argued that economic growth as development should be pursued, but complemented with social development programmes for those who were 'excluded'. This approach did not fare much better, and the idea of socio-economic development, in which social development principles were to be mainstreamed in the economic growth process, was born.

Social development is commonly used to include policies and programmes designed to combat poverty, unemployment, crime, social exclusion, ill health and illiteracy—all noble causes. But noble intentions do not easily produce the desired results; they sometimes produce the opposite. Most social development programmes, in both developed and developing countries, run the risk of fostering the victim mentality, creating dependency and deepening disempowerment, although they seek the reverse.

The 1995 Social Summit in Copenhagen, which addressed the themes of poverty, unemployment and social exclusion, was a significant milestone in the history of development. Apart from its direct outcomes in the form of commitments and an action plan adopted by well over 100 heads of states, the summit raised the political profile of social development. But five years later, while several developing countries managed real improvements in their social development indicators, the problems identified at Copenhagen are still with us and many have worsened. The main reasons for this are the usual one—lack of new and additional resources and lack of political will.

The results of the Social Summit review will be presented at the Special Session of the United Nations General Assembly in Geneva shortly. Hopefully, the Special Session will generate not only innovative solutions, but also the political will to carry them out. The General Assembly three simple and somewhat basic recommendations should be kept in mind:

- Reiterate poverty eradication as the top priority of the international and national development agenda.
- Recommend an operationally enhanced human development strategy as the practical framework for development cooperation for poverty eradication.
- Encourage development agencies and governments to use their existing sectoral mandates as entry points in a synergistic framework provided by the operationally enhanced human development framework, which could also be called a sustainable livelihoods approach.

All of the above are politically and operationally feasible. The implication of the first is to focus on the single theme of poverty eradication for action over the next five years. Social exclusion could be addressed in the strategy for poverty reduction, and employment should be seen as one of the entry points for action in the strategic action framework for poverty eradication. This provides a clear agenda around which political will, resources and action can be mobilised.

The second and third proposals addressed the weaknesses of the welfare and/or growth and trickle down approaches to poverty eradication in current vogue. Such a social agenda creates a no-win situation, in the sense that even when it succeeds in squeezing out some reprieve for workers, the poor and the disadvantaged, it produces more victims waiting to be saved and so fosters a pervasive disempowerment process. Further, and more importantly, the rationale places the economy before people.

The human development approach offers a powerful and viable alternative by fundamentally reversing the premise on which development planning proceeds—to put the economy at the service of the people rather than the reverse. The question then is how to address the social development agenda through an enhanced human development approach?

At the operational, level, the following would greatly enhance the human development approach to poverty eradication:

- Begin by focusing on what people have (the assets approach), not what they need by defining assets broadly to include human, social, national and physical capital.
- Understand people's adaptive strategies to shocks and stresses and seek to further develop and release their creativity by appropriate policy, governance, technology and investment shifts and inputs.
- Mainstream the environment by giving natural capital the same level of importance as human, social and physical capital in the programme design framework.
- Mainstream gender by paying attention to different patterns of asset ownership by men and women and their different adaptive strategies.

On an optimistic note, the evolution of development practice has more often than not been characterized by a willingness to learn from past mistakes and to move forward with new and innovative paradigms. This spirit must continue if the dream of a poverty-free world is to be realised.

24

RICHER OR POORER?

Achievements and Challenges of Ethical Trade

Ethical trade as an approach to supply chain management has mushroomed in recent years. Northern companies are becoming increasingly concerned with the 'ethics' of their operations and the risks to reputation and productivity posed by bad employment practices in global supply chains. But can voluntary private sector codes really improve employment conditions in supply chains?

Ethical trade is one dimension of corporate social responsibility, bringing social issues into the mainstream of commercial supply chain management through the use of codes of conduct. It is sometimes confused with fair-trade which addresses terms of trading for smaller producers, and fosters greater responsibility in supply chain relations.

Ethical trade, on the other hand, focuses on workpalce issues, requiring that supplier's in particular meet minimum employment, worker welfare and aspects of human rights standards.

Similar management systems are well established for product safety and environmental issues, Here, we focus on the social dimensions of ethical trade and its codes of conduct yet the separation of social and environmental standards is increasingly artificial in global sourcing agreements.

A plethora of codes are on offer. The most numerous are in-houses codes such as Nike's 233 company codes were counted in 1999 and the figure is rising.

Suppliers have to comply with and pay for a multitude of similar but different codes. Harmonising codes or establishing equivalence is on the agenda but has not yet halted the problem of 'code overload'.

At a broader level, industry-specific codes have also been developed. The US Apparel industry Partnership/Fair Labour Agreement adopted by a number of leading US merchandising companies is a good example. Industry standards are not new, as ISO and EMAS environmental management systems show. Building on ISO principles, Social Accountability International (formerly CEPAA) has developed SA8000. This is an independent social standard that can be used as an auditable code throughout the private sector.

Ethical trade is partly a response to consumer and campaigning group pressure in globalised economy. Alliances of companies, NGOs, trade. Developing codes of conduct through a multi stakeholder approach is a striking aspect of ethical trade, bringing together companies, NGOs, trade unions and some government departments. An example of this collaborative approach is the Ethical Trading Initiative (ETI) in the UK. The ETI's baseline code of conduct that corporate members for various industries must comply with as a minimum standard is more than just a code, ETI aims to provide a learning environment and sponsors pilot projects in developing countries to test different methods of monitoring and verification.

Codes of conduct need to be assessed in terms of content, implantation and impact. A number of professional auditing companies have moved into this area, some accredited to audit specific codes such as FLA or SA8000. Suppliers audited against a specific code undergo an inspection, and where non-compliance is found, have to take remedial action or risk failing that audit.

Social auditing is a complex process, however, and it can be difficult to spot work place abuse, such as sexual harassment or forced overtime, workers have little confidence in a process that appears to be linked with management, and fear that reporting issues could risk their jobs. Advocates of the multi stakeholder approach argue that effective monitoring and verification of codes must involve local NGOs and trade unions in which workers have trust. Participatory social auditing, also a means of raising awareness and of facilitating behavioural change, can help reveal serious management problems. But in many developing countries local organisations lack the capacity to participate: developing sustainable local systems of monitoring and verification remains an important challenge.

Do the advantages of multi-stakeholder approaches outweigh immediate constraints? Ethical trade is a largely northern driven process, reflecting Western ethical thinking and priorities, Southern based initiatives, however, are expanding, raising the possibility of local ownership of codes, collaboration poses challenges. Stronger relationships and better understanding are essential between southern and northern workers, producers, trade unions, and NGOs for codes to work globally.

But there is still scepticism as to the extent of the benefits that ethical trade might bring. Will increasing southern capacity to participate, as the ETI has done in its pilot project, help? Will building trust, confidence and dialogue achieve the objectives of ethical trade, north and south? Child labour is often more complex, however, than codes make it appear. Codes need to address the conditions of all workers within the supply chain, including the least visible: partnerships must include all groups to address these limitations.

The role of government is hotly contested. Can a system whose credibility depends on under-resourced civil society actors, often excluding democratically elected representatives, maintain genuine credibility? If the boundaries between private sector and public sector roles are not defined, the list of private sector responsibilities will become unmanageable. Private sector initiatives are not a substitute for more comprehensive national or international development policies.

What are the consequences of codes? Do they encourage downsizing or reinforce from large suppliers where compliance is more easily monitored? There is a risk that the gains of some will be at the expense of others.

Ethical trade has successfully begun forging partnerships to find solutions. While it might be wrong to assume that ethical trade can change the world, handled wisely it could make a world of difference for some. Yet it is not a panacea for development. Issues that remain unchallenged by ethical trade include:

- The exclusion of companies producing for domestic markets—often bigger employers.
- Underlying causes of poverty and social marginalisation.

25

AID EFFECTIVENESS AS A MULTI-LEVEL PROCESS

Parallel to the widespread decrease of aid resources provided by donor countries to developing countries in recent years, debate and research on how to make aid more effective has become a major concern of policy makers and donor aid administrators. Usually, it is suggested that decades of development assistance have at best produced mariginal results in terms of improving development levels in the South, Little mention is made of donor's policy shortcomings and the negative impact of these on efforts aimed at reforming and redefining development cooperation in order to enhance aid effectiveness. The policy parameters and operating frame work's of existing aid policies continue to inhibit higher degree of aid effectiveness. In many donor countries, opinion polls indicate waning public support for development aid.

Increasingly, the moral case for aid is called into question and deeper world market integration tends to be seen as the panacea to continued economic decline and social destabilisation in the South. Against this background, cooperation between donor and recipient actors is faced with a dual uphill struggle. First, fewer resources can be mobilised to meet growing developmental needs. On the other hand, to organise and manage development policies and programmes in result oriented manner, grows more difficult.

The threat of further aid cuts and of further drops of public support for providing aid become ever more real. A closer look at the organisational complexities and political constraints under which development cooperation is expected to perform effectively may help to improve current aid management approaches.

Towards Conceptual Clarity

At first, catchy definitions of what constitutes effective aid might appear attractive to use, in particular with regard to economic indicators. The term 'aid effectiveness' is easily used in the same vein as 'efficiency', 'significance' or 'impact' of aid. At times, obsession to measure and demonstrate the results of aid supported development processes can be observed among policy-makers and administrators on the donor side. Still the understanding of aid and its effectiveness as being part and parcel of a cooperation relationship between donor and recipient side parties, is scarcely embedded in practice. To determine how to make aid more effective requires more than a quick impact analysis of an individual and perhaps even isolated developments project, consequently, defining the concept of aid effectiveness needs to take into account at what levels cooperation is focused on. To strive for sustainable and active modes of development cooperation will entail the need to combine recipient ownership of the development process with donor accountability concerns.

Performance expectations cannot be exclusively placed on the recipient while donor interests, their aid management systems and procedures remain unchanged.

An extended and more analytical, process oriented definition should take into account four main aspects of aid effectiveness:

(a) effective aid must relate to the building and/or strengthening of in-country aid management capacity;

(b) to maximise the degree of aid effectiveness, local ownership of the aid process is essential: from setting of priorities through policy formulation and implementation on to the evaluation stages of the process;

(c) increasing recipient side capabilities to take charge of aid relationship, will need to be combined with arrangements to meet legitimate donor accountability concerns;

(d) aid effectiveness is a two-faceted objective: its realisation is equally dependent on increased transparency of donor motives and on dropping of non-developmental, political and economic aid objectiveness of donors.

In addition a broader range of stakeholders in the aid relationship needs to be actively involved: extending beyond accountable government and implementing agencies, to include democratic institutions and organisations of civil society and of the private sector.

Applying any definition of aid effectiveness without desegregating macro-economic data and taking into account country specificity will only lead to unhelpful generalisations about aid and its effectiveness. It would seem more appropriate to adopt working definitions against which to assess effectiveness of aid resources at a country-specific level. On such a basis one could expect to arrive at more reliable indicators of how well aid resources contribute to improving developmental standards and meeting exiting needs.

From Definition to Success—Key Requirements

Having reached agreement between the recipient and donor on what should constitute effectiveness of aid is only a starting point. Embarking on democratic, peaceful and participatory patterns of economic and social development must follow: to arrive at significant and lasting improvements in many of the least developed countries will be a long-term process. This being said, it is crucial to design and implement such forms of development cooperation which involve a wide range of recipient side actors, not only from the government side but also from civil society at large. Seen as a process of increasing inclusion of intended beneficiaries of aid, the commitment to decentralise as well as entrust aid and its management grows in importance.

To fully capture Third World development realities, policy frameworks inspired by neo-liberalist type of development concepts and theories are grossly inadequate. The views and positions on aid articulated in the World Bank and the IMF and others, represent only one side of today's international cooperation, namely the donor side. The major weakness to point out with respect to this locus of debate, is a profound under-representation if not even a total absence of recipient experiences and perceptions on aid in general and on its effectiveness in particular. There should be little doubt that ignoring or not actively identifying and involving such perceptions, leads to strongly donor-driven aid.

To circumvent recipient side insights and views on strengths and weaknesses of aid strategies and mechanisms, will result in limited local commitment and sense of ownership over the aid process. Mutual decision-making between donors and recipients remains a rare policy approach. Aid procedures that are based on local management and less control-oriented donor roles in the aid process are still exceptions in development cooperation.

Structurally, in terms of the policy environment within which development aid is expected to function, the overriding policy framework is generally based on structural adjustment policies (SAP). But the underlying conclusion made by proponents of SAPs that these policies induce aid effectiveness, has yet to be proven valid. It must suffice at this point to emphasize that there is no a priori relationship between world market integration under structural adjustment and sustainable development in poor countries. Aid to these countries which is solely intended to reinforce fundamentally uneven and unequal patterns of world market integration should at be scrutinised critically.

Some central issues need to be addressed in the course of improving aid and its effectiveness:

- Institutional dimensions of aid relationships require strong policy-attention, both on the donor and the recipient side;
- capacities to effectively identify and formulate aid priorities need to be strengthened in recipient countries;
- local capacities to sustain reform efforts must be reinforced.

Levels of Intervention

If the design of aid and the terms upon which it is provided to a developing country are largely determined by the donor, the aid relationship can be characterised as essentially hierarchical. Recipient side views will rarely surface, as they are either not identified, or not well formulated. Possibilities of a recipient-led development strategies can be limited. Unless scope is provided to the recipient side actors to assume responsibilities, aid effectiveness is likely to remain low or fluctuating, and the sustainability of donor aid efforts will remain doubtful.

National planning processes and courses of national development in recipient countries should be seen as most effective where they are led under local responsibility and control. To arrive at this ideal situation, gaps need to be reduced and closed at the various intervention levels.

Donor aid resources provide valuable support for this process. Their effectiveness in meeting longterm objective of aid will need to be assessed on the basis of how well they perform at the different levels. Individual donors will expectedly perform differently at the various levels. What will prove to be the ultimate test for effectiveness is how well the donor aid performance accomplishes the broader objectives of development cooperation and how well it includes sustainable results.

In the analytical framework outlined here, development cooperation would seem to be confronted with the effectiveness gaps at the:

- *structural level:* international trade and investment patterns, debt problems and world market integration processes appear as long-term constraining factors upon aid and its effectiveness;
- *at the policy level,* dialogue and partnership in development cooperation are instrumental factors in recluding planning and coordination gaps with regard to policy analysis and formulation;
- *the institutional level* is where pertinent capacity gaps exist: capacity development efforts of donors and technical assistance measures play an important role in addressing weaknesses in aid effectiveness within a country's institutional setting;
- finally, at the *level of aid projects (programmes),* it is generally the lack of sustainability of aid interventions which causes development activities to falter once donor support decreases or stops, in addition to technical cooperation, financial and material inputs serve to maintain project momentum and goal realisation: the issue of how to develop local capacity sufficiently in order for indigenous organisations to continue project activities initially supported by donor aid, remains the most important issue to address at this level.

Fostering and Effectiveness

In recent years donor aid budgets have been reshuffled, while having decreased in real terms. Geographical redistributions of reduced aid budgets have been accompanied by the need to accommodate rising emergency needs.

Additional resources to meet these needs have not been forthcoming: in general, aid budgets destined for developmental purposes have been under severe pressure while urgent humanitarian needs have added to the drain on resources.

Donor and recipient development efforts are too often isolated from one another, or poorly coordinated. They fail to address managerial and implementation bottlenecks. Cross-sectorial linkages, as well as interdisciplinary approaches to aid problems are only slowly gaining ground. It is increasingly obvious, that decisions on aid issues are subjected to concerns outside to the responsible ministry: finance ministers, economics ministers and unfortunately even defence ministers have a strong say in how much aid is to be provided, where it is to be concentrated and under what terms to be utilised. Inside of recipient countries, large portions of national budgets are allocated to non-development priorities with little or no impact on alleviating urgent poverty problems.

Development cooperation may make the biggest impact and be executed most effectively where donors and recipients agree upon multi-level aid strategies. To give an example: building a road to a remote rural area many well be done in an effective project manner: it is equally important to have a functioning transport authority in place to ensure maintenance of the roads. If this authority operates within a nationally defined infrastructure policy, best in accord with national trade and investment priorities, then the effectiveness of the project-level road building programme has a good chance of being high.

Institutional changes to set the stage for a profound reform process in development cooperation are needed. Re-prioritising national budgets to reflect identified incountry development needs may be one step. Setting up policy evaluation and formulation units can be complimentary measures. Deregulating markets and investment rules may serve to please donors, but dumping of cheap products which strangle local production efforts may easily result. Regional cooperation, including intensified South-South cooperation can provide some counterbalance. There are only a few areas where changes in the current system of development cooperation can occur, with a view to better mange the complexities of aid and the social, cultural economic and political backgrounds against which they take place. The will and commitment to take policy action in both donor and recipient countries, through the broadest range of stakeholders and institutions as possible, will be the test for genuine efforts at improving development relations between North and South and organising cooperation effectively.

26

TAXATION SYSTEMS IN DEVELOPING COUNTRIES

There have been radical changes during the last two decades in the academic assessment of the role of governments in economic development. These include the now widely accepted maxim. "As little government as possible, as much as necessary". The degree of government intervention to be discussed is determined by the role of governments. Fiscal policy, as a part of economic policy, is especially affected. Fiscal policy considerations play an equally pivotal role in taking decisions on economic policy in industrial, developing and transition countries alike. For example, this applies when it comes to reducing unemployment, excessive budget deficits and public debt burdens. Or when national savings rates are too low, or governments seek an answer to the problems of pension and public health systems.

Usually, fiscal policy instruments are differentiated as public spending, tax revenue and the budget balance. The following can be implemented as specific fiscal policy activities to influence the economic stability of the transition and growth process; structural taxation reforms; reform of public spending and debt management; extra-budgetary operations; and changes in the less visible, quasi fiscal activities of state-owned enterprises or financial institutions.

The following observations, however, focus on the importance of taxation policy and the institutions needed to implement it. Aspects of public spending and debt management are highlighted only on the sidelines. A brief analysis of the main problem areas in the developing countries will precede reflections on them.

The Developing Countries' Starting-point

Many Asian countries like India made greater efforts in recent years to allocate public funds effectively. They have thereby paid special attention to reforming budget systems and setting priorities for public spending. Changes in the level and structure of public expenditure, such as government investments, subsides and transfers, can also create general conditions relevant to private sector growth. However, experience in above all the context of structural adjustment programmes shows that successful reform of public budgets also requires reform of the revenue side. Declining budget assistance and low utilisation of existing taxation potential call for a more intensive addressing of the questions of why the public budget is so limited, and how tax-induced economic distortions can be corrected. Summing up, the problems in the government revenue sector can be identified as:

- dependency of taxation on international trade;
- low incomes (subsistence economy, informal sector);
- opaque taxation systems (exemption rules, small tax base, high tax rates);
- lack of economic incentives;
- unequal taxation (unequal treatment of ordinary and judicial people);
- inefficient administrations;
- ponderous administrative procedures;
- hierarchical administrative action;
- low taxpayer honesty;

- political resistance by influential interest groups;
- corruption.

Influence of Taxation Policy on General Economic Development

Taxation policy aspects such as tax structure, design of individual taxes, over-all scope of taxation and taxation administration can in many ways directly influence the allocation of resources, the stability of the economy, and distribution of income, and thus affect growth. Finally, almost every tax provokes a change of behaviour of the economic entity, which leads to wrong allocations and can result in a loss of social services.

Switching from income tax to a tax on consumption, for example, can impact positively on saving behaviour, and thus trigger greater accumulation of capital. Whereas using income as the tax base rewards consumption and penalises saving (deferred consumption), this does not apply to a tax on personal spending. Empirical studies, however, do not make clear whether the savings level depends on taxation and if so in what form.

Rather, it can be assumed that taxation merely influences the savings structure. Besides that, it must be seen that greater savings do not automatically lead to growth. Using the savings for investments calls for complementary factors such as functioning foreign exchange and finance markets.

Tax incentives such as so-called tax expenditure (which can be offset against tax) to promote investment and R&D can also have a significant influence on allocation of resources and technological progress. The impacts of tax reductions on growth depend on whether and what public spending is cut at the same time. If there are no cuts, the budget deficit can lead to rising interest rates, and thus have a negative influence on growth.

There are reservations with respect to the effectiveness of Tax-induced effects on growth. Equally, social and industrial policy goals such as promotion of investment and R&D are to be questioned. However, developing countries in particular fall back in large measure of instrument of tax expenditure. Introducing such tax breaks bears the risk that the taxation system will be even more opaque and the tax base eroded. In the case of a given amount of revenue, this results in tax rates for the remaining taxpayers having to be raised. This, in turn, reinforces economic distortions. Moreover, such taxation policy measures can also incur politico-economic costs. They are often accompanied by sinecure-seeking behaviour, corruption and the forming of interest groups, which as a whole can inhibit growth.

Finally, uncertainty over future fiscal or taxation policy can have equally negative impacts on investment and thus growth. Among other things, this can be created by inflationary tendencies or opaque and inconsistent political decision-making processes, which are now customary in many developing countries. Planning security in particular is very important in creating a climate which encourages investment.

On the whole, the international tax reduction competition that goes with globalisation of markets can lead to decreases in growth. The degree to which countries are tempted to attract international customers of foreign capital by cutting taxes and vying with each other in lowering their taxation levels can also reduce revenues and consequently public spending on infrastructure or social services.

A taxation policy aimed at promoting growth should therefore be designed to achieve broadest taxation neutrality. That means tax-induced distortions of resources allocation should be minimised so far a possible in line with given revenue requirements. This can be achieved mainly in the direct taxation sector of income and corporation tax by a distinct reduction of individual tax rates and simultaneous widening of the tax base, extensive scrapping of tax breaks and exemptions, and equal treatment in taxing the government, non-government, private and business sectors. In the developing countries the current taxation method contributes on average only 25-30 per cent of revenue. Essentially, this can be attributed to practical application problems-poor book-keeping and billing, and of the informal sector high proportion of the tax base.

The share of indirect taxation in total revenue is very high in the developing countries. Traditionally, this can be credited to import and export duties. But the price distortions they induce and the heavy dependence of government revenues on external factors such as world trade prices and volumes impact negatively on the countries macro-economic balance and competitiveness. Consumer taxes in general are characterised by extensive exemptions, taxation at point-of-production, and insufficient registering of the tax base. That is why the taxation system should essentially hinge on a broad tax base that has few exemptions, features indirect taxation in the form of a Value Added Tax on end-consumers, and contains only a few traditional purchase taxes.

It should be emphasised, however, that precisely in developing countries, the design of a taxation system must guarantee a minimum degree of social justice. This can be achieved, for example, by exempting minimum degree of social justice. This can be achieved, for example, by exempting minimum wages or reducing the VAT rate on daily necessities. A regressive taxation effect is to be avoided.

A consistent taxation system, equal taxation, and a stable political situation are essential prerequisites in developing countries for establishing a taxation system that is as neutral and predictable as possible, creates an investment-friendly climate, and at the same time guarantees the financing of important government services.

These guidelines for a taxation policy targeted on economic growth are in most cases followed only insufficiently in developing countries. Typically, as already mentioned, their taxation systems are characterised by a high degree of complexity and opaqueness, low tax yields, and hostility between taxpayers and administrations. Designers of reforms should also bear in mind whether the available government institutions are able to enforce them. In many developing countries, that calls for a simple taxation system which focuses on indirect taxation and pay-as-you-earn (PAYE) tax, and thus takes account of the poor capacity of the implementing institutions.

Importance of the Implementing Institutions

A consistent material taxation law aligned on the market economy does not inevitably lead to an improved fiscal policy situation in many developing countries. The economic policy objectives laid down in the taxation laws can be successfully implemented only if the people and taxation administration are willing and able to apply the laws.

For this reason, taxation reform must take account of local conditions such as the communication infrastructure and capacity of the administration. Only in this way can it be guaranteed that planned changes are really also applied. Problems of a lack of training, opaqueness of administrative action, and corruption can result in the intended political objectives being counteracted in implementation. Extensive reforms of taxation policy and the budgetary and public spending side have been undertaken in recent years. But studies have proven that reforms were successful only in those countries in which the appropriate organisational, staff and material prerequisites for implementing them were in place, and a comprehensive reform approach was selected.

In this sense, linking taxation policy and tax administration, and public spending and budget systems, in developing and transition countries has a special importance. This finding is also supported by experience in the context of stabilisation and structural adjustment programmes of the IMF and World Bank. Un-realistic assessment of administrative capacities was one of the main causes of the failure of many taxation policies in developing countries. An orderly administration that is based on legal foundations and renounces arbitrary action is of decisive importance for creating a climate for promoting development in the private sector.

The inefficiency of taxation administrations can have various causes. On the one hand, they can be due to taxation law, and on the other hand the taxation administration itself can be at fault because it often lacks resources, professional staff and a clear strategy. This is aggravated by the fact that as a government revenue collection authority, the taxation administration is especially at risk to corruption. And that, differing from culture to culture, can be very marked.

Experience shows that regardless of a country's culture, the efficiency of taxation administration can be improved if the right country-specific incentives and institutions are employed and established, and administrative reform is sure of open and durable political support.

The poor capacities of administrations frequently result in a lack of efficiency and effectiveness in tax collection.

That means the available tax potential is insufficiently utilised. The main causes are:

- inefficient organisational structures and processes;
- lack of know-how within the administrations;
- insufficient registration of taxpayers;
- lack of information and monitoring systems;
- lack of acceptance by taxpayers, and often poorly motivated staff.

These negative points are also the key areas of cooperation to strengthen the efficiency of administrations. Questions of the organisation of building administrative capacities and procedures and processes, training, staff leadership, automation, and enlightening taxpayers are the focus. In the context of reform of taxation administrations, value should be placed on tax compliance, such as improving it by effective public relations work and at the same time establishing efficient tax enforcement.

A close meshing of the political and administrative advisory services is necessary to ensure durable and successful reform of the entire taxation system. Doing so will highlight and take account of the feedback effects between taxation policy and taxation administration, which are linked by the material taxation law. They operate in politically sensitive area, and therefore require special harmonisation with the partners. Successful implementation can be guaranteed only with the necessary will to reform on the side of the partner government. Moreover, reforms in government revenue systems should not be seen in isolation. They should be tied into reform of public spending policy and the budgetary system, as well as trade and monetary policy. Only comprehensive approaches to reform which take account of the interdependencies between the individual political areas can pursue a joint macro-economic strategy.

27

THE DEMATERIALISATION OF THE WORLD ECONOMY

The first Industrial Revolution marked the transition from robber-and-plunder colonialism to the systematic development of the 'overseas' territories in the framework of an international division of labour between raw materials suppliers and manufacturers of finished goods. There was an 'historic integration' of the colonised areas in the development of their parent-states. What will the third Industrial Revolution do for the Third World? Will it now come to an 'historic separation'?

The end of the East-West conflict was reason enough to talk about a radical change in world politics. But at the same time an upheaval in the world economy is taking place that possibly will have even wider impacts. As a reference point for the following thoughts, three dimensions of this change are pointed out;

1. The upgrading of processing information rather than materials as object of economic activity (technological dimension);
2. the evolvement of global communications networks (socio-cultural dimension);
3. the change of the nature of work (socio-economic dimension).

All three dimensions can be summarised under the buzzphrase "tertialisation of the world economy".

In that respect, talk of the "Third Industrial Revolution" is misleading. It is not about a third epoch of industrialisation, but about the beginning of a de-industrialisation, the transition from the industrial to the information society.

Historic Separation?

In the 1960s and early 1970s, there was often talk of the Third World as the Third Sector of the world economy. Also then the Third World was not much more than an 'imaginary community'. But as such it had a certain significance in world politics. This implied not only its strategic role in the East-West conflict and its ideological function as the supporter of different 'third paths' between capitalism and socialism. It was also about the Third World's attested 'chaos power'. That linked the fear (in the North) and the hope (in the South) that the developing countries would be in a position to cut off the industrial nations from supplies of important raw materials, thus putting them under pressure. But it was soon seen that both sides had over estimated this possibility, even with regard to oil. Instead of supply bottlenecks arising, raw materials prices plumeted. For some commodities, the fall in prices exceeded those of the Great Depression of 1929/30.

This was due, inter alia, to the conjunction of lower demand from the industrial nations and expansion of production by the raw materials suppliers. Business activities dependent upon the supply of raw materials are tending to lose importance compared with the overall development of the global economy. The reason for this is to be seen in the transition from a material to an information economy.

This transition is taking place in line with the revolutionising of data transmission and the expansion of financial transactions which are not directly related to changes in the production of materials. The speed of the changes is remarkable.

However, the dematerialisation of business activities does not lead to decoupling of the Third World from the world economy. Declining market shares in world trade are not the expression of separation, but a loss of the affected countries positions in the world economy. Thus, the impact of dematerialisation is "only" that the negotiating positions of raw materials suppliers vis-a-vis the industrial nations will deteriorate further.

Differentiation of the Third World

But the radical change in the global economy is affecting some developing countries worse than others. Sub-saharan Africa, and some countries in West and South Asia and Latin America are being pushed back further. The oil-producing countries with their high per capita export earnings will be able to hold their positions in the world economy for some time to come. The threshold countries of East and South-East Asia can expand theirs so long as they can continue to attract a growing share of global industrial production, and at the same time participate in the tertialisation of the world economy in the shape of rapidly-growing financial transactions. Thereby it should be noted that the degree of tertialisation in itself is not an adequate indicator for economic avant-gardism. Brazil exhibits a high degree of tertialisation in combination with a low macro-economic development dynamics. A good part of its tertialisation is being achieved by speculative financial transactions with their inherently greater risks and uncertainties than in the industrial countries. Such dangers have been demonstrated by Mexico's peso crisis and its repercussions on the whole of Latin America.

In some Third World countries, a 'location annuity' has replaced the old raw materials one. Here it's about providing locations for off-shore transactions which offer international capital traders a maximum of freedom of movement combined with low taxation. Suitable for such operations are small countries which, despite low levy rates, achieve significant income in macro-economic terms.

The radical changes in the world economy are spurring the differentiation of the Third World without, however, necessarily fostering a dissolution of the Third World as an 'imaginary community'. It is precisely the advanced countries of East and South-East Asia that are showing a certain interest in the formulation of joint positions of the 'South' in order to secure their own positional gains in the global economy. It's not by chance that the non-aligned countries and the Group of 77 have formed a joint coordination committee, and that the ASEAN countries are changing course on the international human rights policy.

Hitherto, the developing countries' strategy was to broaden the concept of human rights as a justification for demands on the industrial nations. But of late some developing countries, led by the ASEAN states, have questioned the universal validity of human rights even after their universality was confirmed by consensus at the Conference on Human Rights in Vienna in 1993. Playing a role in this policy is the governments' fear that due to the expansion of global communications networks, the behaviour patterns and preferences of their own people could in some way become similar to those of the West. As the rulers see it, that would be detrimental to the continuation of the development models practised so far.

Internet Creates New Cultural Dimension

Much information which Asian governments view as subversive is already globally available on the Internet. The old struggle over the world information order, which at first was primarily a clinch between East and West, is thus taking on a new dimension. For with the growing importance of computer literacy to a country's ability to assert itself on world markets, the Asian threshold countries have not only an interest in controlling the on-line communication but also to expand it and the know-how that it requires.

Even the critics of any interventions in the internet and other global communications networks must admit that modern communications technologies are politically blind and their use in itself does not represent progress. The setting up and expansion of global information highways will offer forum not only to people who want to use it for education and enlightenment, but also to all shades of fundamentalists. These highways will not necessarily bring the misery of many Third World regions closer to the industrial countries, but possibly rather strengthen the tendency to process all world events as entertainment.

Global Two-thirds Society

The gravest aspect of the current upheaval in the world economy is its negative impact on jobs. The information economy needs for fewer workers than an economy based on materials. Instead, the demands on the skills of the workers are growing. Twenty per cent of the world workforce will in future be employed as (overworked) 'intelligence workers'. Eighty per cent will work part-time, if they are not underemployed or jobless. So the tertialisation of the global economy delivers more underemployment rather than more leisure time. The workers who are rationalised out of their jobs in the industrial sector cannot be absorbed by the service sector because it, too, is not left untouched by rationalisation measures. The civil service is also cutting back on staff. At all levels, there's a race to make the greatest possible savings on payrolls. At the same time, there's growing pressure to cut costs in providing for the victims of this development. That means thinning out the social security safety net.

The bottom line is that the two-thirds society, which developmental action groups hitherto assumed was limited to the Third World, is spreading worldwide. That, however, will not in the foreseeable future lead to an amendment of the North-South disparities. It's true that the change in the global economy is taking place faster and to a greater extent in the industrial nations. But rationalisation is also happening in the developing countries in a bid to boost their competitiveness. So the upheaval in the world economy aggravates the problems which exist in a majority of the developing countries, while creating new ones in the industrial nations. The need for action on the North-South policy is growing, while the industrial nations. The need for action on the North-South Policy is growing, while the industrial nations' scope for concessions and compromises is shrinking. The new social question which is now crystallising at global level is not being answered. The consequences are unforeseeable.

Another Loser?

It's more probable that a sharpening of the North-South confrontation is to be reckoned with. For the industrial nations will attempt to keep the social costs of the information economy at bay for as long as possible. The trade unions will thereby compete with the developing countries for jobs for their members. But this policy has its limits precisely because of the peaking of the problems in the industrial nations. Overstepping these limits means war, and passively accepting them chaos and social decay. Solutions could be sought in two directions: effective taxation of the information economies, and the creation of jobs in the non-profit sector. But it's possible there are no global solutions for global problems. That would mean for at least part of the Third World a renewal of the old debate on partial decoupling from the world economy.

28

SOLVING THE UNEMPLOYMENT PROBLEM BY LOOKING BEYOND THE JOB

If you had a job, you worked; if you didn't you didn't. Having a job meant being employed by an organisation in a clearly-defined and stable occupational role, with duties, hours, rates of pay and promotion all more or less standardised. But the job—in that meaning of the world—is a social invention, and a fairly recent one.

The job—the kind that you had, or hoped to get—became a central fixture of life. Its importance was great because it served many needs: For managers and efficiency experts, job assignments were the key to assembly-line manufacturing. For union organizers, jobs protected the rights of workers. For political reformers, standardized civil service positions were the essence of good government. Jobs provided an identity to immigrants and recently-urbanised farm workers. They provided a sense of security for individuals and an organising principle for society.

Jobs functioned in so many ways that it is surprising how many organisations are now opting for other ways to define and manage work. The second job shift is underway. Its emergence can be seen in the increasing use of temporary and part-time workers and contracted-out services, the changing relationship between workers and management, the growing popularity of self-employment and small business. Indeed, 'de-jobbing' is proceeding at such a pace that many economists, management experts and futurists are now talking freely about the end of the job. Bridges predicts that the job as we now know it will disappear entirely—replaced by new kinds of flexible work assignments in post-job organisations—and be remembered only as a quaint artefact of the industrial age.

One reason for the change in work is the economic rules of the survival game among organisations that employ workers. To stay successful in today's hi-tech consumer economy, businesses have had to re-model themselves into what some experts call 'agile companies'—ones that are able to respond quickly to conditions in ever-changing, fragmenting, competitive markets.

The 'knowledge worker', whose work involves not simply doing something, but also applying theoretical or analytical skills. Such workers are replacing the industrial labourer as the dominant part of the workforce—and their productive activities likely to be organised and structured much differently from those of their assembly-line predecessors.

De-jobbing as a result of new technology or the emergence of a service economy is a phenomenon that gets a lot of attention these days; but it is not the whole story. At all levels of society, people are improvising livelihoods that do not fit the industrial-era model. Immigrants to the developed countries, often unable to find steady jobs, nevertheless find places in the new landscape by being mobile, flexible, resourceful and imaginative: they moonlight, work part-time, share jobs, start small businesses. Their lives are often extremely difficult, but they are also instructive to those of us who believe you either have a job or you're out of luck.

It is too early to evaluate the implications of this multifaceted transformation of work, or to dismiss it as simply good or bad. Nevertheless, one cannot deny that it is taking place, and will bring about dramatic social changes.

On the downside, the job shift is causing great hardships for many workers and their families. It poses serious challenges to policy-makers, political activists and labour leaders. The basic question appears to be whether the key to global employment—development strategy is to play 'catch-up'—trying to bring millions of people around the world into jobs in industries and the public sector; or to play 'leapfrog'—creating new forms of employment.

The proposal to generate more employment in agriculture, for example, is based on new demand for agricultural exports from developing countries. The policies designed to make the most of this opportunity include measures to upgrade technology, raise productivity, ensure the supply of essential inputs, establish marketing and distribution channels, create links between agriculture and industry, and cater to export markets.

The issue of part-time work, another kind of employment that is seriously undervalued in the traditional industrial-era job mind-set. Part-time work may not offer much at this point to developing countries, where many people are under employed and wages are low, but it can be of great help in more advanced economies. And it is likely to be a big part of the global work picture in the years ahead.

A certain agility may also be necessary in agriculture, particularly in countries that for many years have depended heavily on producing commodities such as sugar for export as a means of generating income and employment. As Northern laboratories develop non—agricultural substitutes for many of these commodities—and this is already beginning to happen—the bottom may fall out of 'monoculture' economies, only economic, but will have long-run political implications as communities attempt to reorganize themselves in response to the changed conditions. It is, therefore, in the interest of raw materials exporters to closely monitor current trends in biotechnology and the use of genetic resources and modify their internal policies in anticipation of potential long-term effects.

This calls for flexibility, and an ability to get information and to act on it. Government officials, development workers, community leaders and individuals will, in some respects, all have to be 'knowledge workers' if they are to keep ahead of global changes. Jobs are going to be created not just by putting people to work, but by finding—or creating—new niches where they can be productive.

It is still possible to talk about jobs for all, and to resist the assumption made by many economists that high levels of employment are now inevitable. But, as we move ahead into the global information economy, we may be moving back into an older conception of the job, and seeing it again as something you do, rather than as something you have—or that has you.

29
CRISIS AND NEW ORIENTATION OF DEVELOPMENT POLICY

The poverty in the South, the dislocations in the East, and the orientation crisis in the North are not isolated phenomena. Rather, they represent an alarming amalgamation of dangers that are globally interlinked.

The low effectiveness of international economic and development policy is rooted in two outdated paradigms on which the present worldwide strategy of economic development is based, namely that:

1. The Western social and economic model optimises the activation of productive forces—independent of the development stage of a country and its culture and therefore is best suited to satisfy basic needs.

2. It is possible to launch the development of a society from the outside within a few decades—without regard to its cultural and historical background—through external input of money, goods, technology, expertise, and personnel.

The twin paradigms of the timelessness and transferability combined with cultural ecological, and financial restrictions—have led international cooperation and development down the wrong path.

Only if we acknowledge the true dimensions of the global dangers, if we recognise the limitations and shortcomings of existing political instruments, and identify outdated theories and contradictory special interests, can we outline the cornerstones of a new policy of global cooperation.

Cornerstones of a New Development Policy

Starting with critical review of the shortcomings and paradigms of the prevailing development strategy, the following Nine cornerstones of a new development policy are offered for discussion:

1. Broaden the Concept of Development

Whether a society is considered developed depends on the size of its per capita Gross National Product (GNP). Accordingly, the world is divided into a developed, semi-developed, and underdeveloped world. The yardstick for development, which has become the norm in the industrial countries, is one-dimensional: It only measures the monetary value of goods and services that are exchanged in the marketplace. This standard is too narrow economically because it compresses the multitude and complexity of cultural, societal, historical, social, and human values into a single economic category.

At the most, there can and should be agreement on what development and progress should not bring about: Inability to find enough work to meet the most basic needs; exploitation and oppression of people; loss of cultural wealth and institutions; destruction of natural resources. These, however, are the very values that are sacrificed by the prevailing development strategy. In the future, development policy must do all it can to stop the loss of skills and self-reliance, the plunder of natural resources, the erosion of cultural values, the violation of human dignity and human rights. Initiatives must prevail which are oriented on these values, and not just on the GNP.

2. Concentrate Development Strategy on the Internal Potential of Developing Countries

There must be an end to the manic fixation of development strategy on external inputs and external markets. A new development policy must, above all, improve internal conditions for a productive economy, promote domestic production factors on a broad basis, protect cultural and natural resources, and greatly increase the domestic supply of basic goods. Wherever external inputs are unavoidable, credits must be strictly tied to the productivity and the ability of a country to absorb transfers. External transfers should be concentrated on 'Software' for health, education, social participation, administrative, and legal jurisdiction. Such an approach could also promote training and indigenous technologies, which are so important for economic development.

The set-up and expansion of the productive sectors must be decided, planned, and implemented by the developing countries themselves, and they must assume full responsibility. The external pressures, which force the developing countries into full integration with the world market, must be removed. This presupposes a structural reduction of interest rates.

3. Make Development Policy a Central Feature of Politics

Development policy must take the lead in mobilising the various political forces and government departments to join the fight against the growing global dangers. It must ensure that the actions of all political departments are compatible with development policy is possible only if it becomes the central task of all political sectors, comparable to social and environmental policies, and the central goal of all policies. If development policy is to become a central task, development problems must become a priority in parliament and government. Society must understand that it is in the national interest to accept great global responsibilities.

4. Reform the World Economy

The industrial countries must abolish their protectionism in agriculture as well the processed goods sector. Simultaneously, the developing countries need to be protected selectively and for a limited time against imports from the industrial countries. The undifferentiated structural adjustment policies imposed by the IMF must be revised. The trend toward regionalisation of the world economy should not be opposed; rather, in the interest of both South and East, it must be regulated constructively to form a new, regionally based world trade structure.

A reform of the international finance system is urgently needed: Interest and exchange rates should not mirror the national interests of the big industrial states and the special interests of large banks and venture capital. Rather, they must reflect the global interest in monetary stability lower and stable interest rates, and sufficient development financing.

However, strengthening the international financial institutions is in the global interest only if the countries of the southern and eastern hemispheres are allowed to exert some influence. An international financial court must guarantee that violations of strict regulations to ensure international stability and solvency can be protested in a court of law.

5. Redesign the Industrial Society

As a global social and environmental policy, the new development policy must induce the industrial countries to give up their excessive consumption of air, water, soil, resources, and space. Increased utilisation of energy-conservation measures and environmental-friendly technologies is overdue. The economic and social policies of the industrial nations must promote balance rather than growth. This requires radical changes in traditional economic thinking, habits, structures and processes.

In view of limited world resources, unsatisfied existential needs in South and East, and continuous population growth in the South must be higher than in the North, but they should no longer be in the North, but they should no longer be induced primarily by growth in the North. If economic policies continue to call for the North to provide the locomotive, the North will have to continue to acquire more resources than the South.

The North must relinquish the remaining growth frontiers to the South and East. The South must use this opportunity to activate its internal dynamic potential rather than integrate its economy with the North. However, ecological and social controls must be established at a much earlier stage than was the case in Europe.

6. Strengthen Development Cooperation

The share of official development assistance as a percentage of GNP, which dropped from 0.48 per cent in 1982 to 0.34 per cent in 1995 must be gradually raised again and reach at least 0.7 per cent in the year 2000—a goal which OECD established as early as two decades ago and which was reconfirmed at the Rio Earth Summit.

However, we must not succumb to the illusion that a doubling of ODA funds will even remotely meet the financial needs of South and East. State development policy must use its scarce public funds more effectively in the future. It must use restraint whenever partners in the developing countries can accomplish a task on their own and private initiatives and private enterprise are more competent to do the job. The government should be directly engaged only when it can be relatively more productive. Otherwise, it should limit itself to subsidizing private organisations.

7. New Orientation for Development Cooperation

The state and its implementation agencies must abandon all direct responsibility for any projects which require unbureaucratic action, economic efficiency, and long term productivity. It must make a much greater effort to involve

NGO's and private venture capital in development projects. At the same time, the state must insist and guarantee that private actions are compatible with social and ecological concerns.

In the future, the main thrust of government projects should be the promotion of the international potential of a country. This comprises the political and administrative frame work conditions of a humane, socially and ecologically sound development: Constitutional government, social institutions which facilitate broad participation of the population in politics, society, and economy; efficient savings, credit, fiscal and financial systems; mechanisms for income, property, and land distribution which promote productivity, justice, and social peace. In addition of this 'software' of development, the following is needed: A regime for the protection of resources and environment; measures to prevent the short term sell-out of natural resources; elementary and general education and training, health care and social safety nets capacities to develop science and technology.

8. Reduce the Debt Service and Activate Private Capital

Public funds must be used to a greater degree for the financial rehabilitation of highly indebted countries in South and East; external demands for interest and principal payments must be adapted to the economic capacity of the respective country and its ability to execute external capital transfers.

Within the framework of international insolvency regulations, initiatives must be developed as a conditions for the continuance of the present rules for write-offs—which ensure effective cooperation from the banks and alleviate the heavy burden of private credits, with their high interest rates.

State development policy and private business interests should supplement each other. Government promotion of private enterprise initiatives for exports, investment, and employment in the developing countries must take into account their compatibility with development. In reverse, private engagements which effectively promote development must be actively supported by the government. A separate line item must be established in the development budget for such activation of private capital.

9. Set Regional Priorities

State development cooperation has been scattering its scarce funds not only among too many sectors, but also among too many partners. In the future, public funds must be concentrated regionally. More emphasis must be placed on regional programmes, and development cooperation with threshold countries must be enhanced. A portion of public funds should be set aside to provide an incentive for be set aside to provide an incentive for threshold countries to assist the poorer nations in their own region as well as deal with poverty in their own country.

The new development policy could then also help lessen ethnic-national conflicts and promote peace by sponsoring regional cooperation in joint development projects. For this purpose, regional development funds must be set up for cooperation in the transportation, energy, trade, and finance sectors and last, but not least for regional security systems and disarmament. Such regional funds could also provide the means to project refugees and improve their prospects for an eventual return to their homelands.

30

TOO MANY RICH PEOPLE

Concern about population problems among citizens of rich countries generally focusses on rapid population growth in most poor nations. But the impact of humanity on Earth's life support systems is not just determined by the number of people alive on the planet. It also depends on how those people behave. When this is considered, an entirely different picture emerges; the main population problem is in wealthy countries. There are in fact, too many rich people.

The amount of resources each person consumes, and the damage done by the technologies used to supply them, need to be taken as much into account as the size of the population. Unhappily, governments do not keep statistics that allow the consumption and technology factors to be readily measured—so scientists substitute per capita energy consumption to give a measure of the effect each person has on the environment.

Using and Consuming

This makes sense. All human activities require the use of energy, and the most environmentally destructive of those activities for the most part require a great deal of it. Human-beings use energy to obtain resources, process them into useful items, and then use or consume them. At every step environmental damage is done.

In traditional societies—more or less in balance with their environments—that damage may be self-repairing. Wood cut for fires or structures regrows, soaking up the carbon dioxide produced when it was burned. Water extracted from streams is replaced by rainfall. Soils in fields are regenerated with the help of crop residues and animal manures. Wastes are broken down and reconverted into nutrients by the decomposer organisms of natural eco-systems.

At the other end of the spectrum, paving over fields and forests with concrete and asphalt, mining the coal and iron necessary for steel production with all its associated land degradation, and building and operation automobiles, trains and aeroplanes that spew pollutants into the atmosphere, are all energy-intensive processes. So are drilling for and transporting oil and gas, producing plastics, manufacturing chemicals (from DDT and synthetic nitrogen fertilisers to chlorofluorocarbons and laundry detergents) and building power plants and dams. Industrialised agriculture uses enormous amounts of energy—for ploughing, planting, fertilising and controlling weeds and insect pests, and for harvesting, processing, shipping, packing, storing and selling foods. So does industrialised forestry for timber and paper production.

Paying the Price

Incidents such as Chernobyl and oil spills are among the environmental prices paid for mobilising commercial energy-and soil erosion, destrtification, acid rain, global warming, destruction of the ozone layer and the toxification of the entire planet are among the costs of using it.

In all, humanity's high-energy activities amount to a large-scale attack on the integrity of Earth's eco-systems and the critical services they provide. These include control of the mix of gases in the atmosphere (and thus of the climate); running of the hydrologic cycle which brings us dependable flows of fresh water; generation and maintenance of fertile soils; disposal of wastes; recycling of the nutrients essential to agriculture and forestry; control of the vast majority of potential crop pests; pollination of many crops; provision of food from the sea; and maintenance of a vast genetic library from which humanity has already withdrawn the very basis of civilisation in the form of crops and domestic animals.

The Relative Impact

The relatively small population of rich people accounts for roughly two-thirds of global environmental destruction, as measured by energy use. From this perspective, the most important population problem is overpopulation in the industrialised nations.

The United States poses the most serious threat of all to human life support systems. It has a gigantic population, the third largest on Earth, more than a quarter of a billion people. Americans are superconsumers, and use inefficient technologies to feed their appetites. Each, on average, uses 11kw of energy, twice as much as the average Japanese, more than three times as much as the average Spaniard, and over 100 times as much as an average Bangladeshi. Clearly, achieving an average family size of 1.5 children in the United States (which would still be larger than the 1.3 child average in Spain) would benefit the world much more than a similar success in Bangladesh.

The reduction in energy consumption could be achieved with technologies already in hand given the necessary political will—and would produce an increase in the quality of life. This would provide room for needed economic growth in poor nations, which could triple their per-person energy use to 3kW. Thus the gap between rich and poor nations would be closed, while the total world impact would increase from 13TW to 30TW (10 billion x 3kW).

Will the environment a century hence be able to support 2.3 times as much activity as today? It's questionable, but perhaps with care it could, at least temporarily. Success would require a degree of cooperation, care for our fellow human beings, and respect for the environment that are nowhere evident now. But society has shown it can change rapidly when the time is ripe.

31
PEOPLE AS HOSTAGES

The Humanitarian Consequences of Sanctions

Following the end of the Cold War, the UN was able to rediscover and impose the sanctions provided for by Article 41 of an UN Charter to maintain or restore international peace and security. Whereas during the preceding decades the UN Security Council had applied such non-military coercive measures only twice, against Rhodesia and South Africa, sanctions have been imposed more than ten times since 1989. The targets: Iraq, Yugoslavia, Somalia, Liberia, Libya, Haiti, Angola, Rwanda, Sudan, Afghanistan, and Sierra Leone. There is now enough experience of the useful and harmful impacts of sanctions to be able to assess the feasibility of this instrument and suggest reforms. That applies also to the bilateral sanctions imposed by the USA.

The Impact of Sanctions

The application of sanctions is at first accompanied with hopes, which are followed mostly by disappointment and sometimes by abhorrence. The hopes are based on the belief that sanctions still can prevent an armed conflict by making a targeted country drop its belligerent attitude due to its leaders listening to reason or responding to the pressure of their people. Disappointment arises from the unreliable calculation of political success, from considerations of legitimacy, and from the problems of affected third countries.

Abhorrence is triggered by the ethical dilemma that the suffering caused by sanctions has a greater impact on the ordinary people than upon the political elite, making them hostages to the confrontation.

To be sure, the UN organs, the Security Council is a political rather than a judical or humanitarian organ of the international community. It does not have to observe the principle of equal treatment and can react differently to developments in Haiti than to those in Nigeria or Burma, to say nothing about Chechnya. But like all UN organs, the Security Council is bound to overarching principles. These include in particular respect for human rights, which it must bear in mind in considering the consequences of its actions.

From a developmental viewpoint, it is worrying to note that sanctions are targeted almost solely on countries of the South. That is just as questionable as the damage suffered by the neighbours and trade partners of countries undersanctions. That applies, for instance, to the Danube littoral states in the case of Yugoslavia, and to Jordan in the case of the sanctions against Iraq.

Furthermore, one of the other drawbacks in wielding the sanctions instrument is the long-standing practice of imposing them on a open-ended basis. That means a country can rid itself of sanctions only with great effort because the veto of a single permanent member of the Security Council can prevent them from being lifted. If sanctions were in future imposed for fixed periods, it would require a fresh Security Council decision to reapply them. Given this process, the sanctions against Libya, for example, would have ended much earlier.

Finally, it is hard to bear that some major powers instrumentalise the Security Council for their own purposes, such as the USA in its quarrel with Libya. Leading Western new media covering the Lockerbie trial in The Netherlands were mean while drip-feeding their publics with selective information from secret service circles to prepare them for the news that Libyan involvement in the bomb blast which brought down the Pan Am airliner over Scotland was unlikely to be proven.

Discussion in the UN

The recommendations of UN secretaries-general for many years for more care in applying the sanctions instrument correspond to a widely-held view in the UN. For instance, Boutros Boutros-Ghali called in his annex to the UN's Agenda for Peace of January 1995 for a "mechanism" to assess and examine the consequences of sanctions. And in Kofi Annan's Millennium Report of April 2000, he called on the UN heads of state and government leaders to agree on measures to make economic sanctions adopted by the Security Council impact less harshly on innocent populations, and more effective in bringing pressure to bear on target regimes. The international Red Cross and other humanitarian aid Organisations have for years made similar statements.

First and foremost, it is about avoiding so-called humanitarian consequences. In 1997 the UN did, in fact, cancel implementation of an agreed flight ban against Sudan due to an expert report which forecast such impacts. That is distinct progress. It also shows that as a rule it is not a matter of unforeseen or unintended impacts in the sense of 'collateral damage'. But about the acceptance of foreseeable and deliberate consequences. For in contrast to the rules of warfare, which primarily should not be waged against the civil population, the logic of sanction impacts is based on their intended effect on the people of the target country. Their morale is to be broken, making them exert internal pressure on their rulers.

The Case of Iraq

Humanitarian consequences arise above all when comprehensive economic sanctions are imposed which, as in the cases of Iraq and Yugoslavia, ban international trade, transport and financial transactions. That means infant and child mortality, hunger, sickness and human misery: impacts that are visibly and measurably a danger to life.

Certainly, causality in individual cases is an area of dispute. Iraq is a clear example of that. The sanctions against it are effecting a population that in a short time have lived through two terrible and bloody wars involving heavy losses, and whose ruler obviously does not give top priority to the immediate basic needs of his people. So there is more than one reason for the misery. But mutual apportioning of blame can exculpate no-one. Whoever creates conditions that cause innocent children to die cannot with a clear conscience claim that others have done that too. The US and Iraqi governments, however, are so deeply hostile to each other than even taking an objective view of the situation in the interest of the people affected is judged as taking sides.

At any rate, sanctions contribute a great deal to worsen a people's plight. Unfortunately, the international debate on sanctions tends so settle for demanding a guarantee of access of humanitarian aid. The Security Council resolutions contain corresponding exemption provisions. Demarcations in the sector of 'dual use' goods have also become somewhat more sensible since the days when Winston Churchill argued that war material could be made even from food. Foodstuffs and medical supplies are expected from the embargo. But that does not solve the humanitarian problem. As we unfortunately note constantly, the aid available around the world is not enough to provide sufficient help in all emergency and disaster situations. That means that people of an internationally outlawed country can expect even less assistance.

An especially annoying circumstance in the case of Iraq was that its own rich resources were not allowed to be used for emergency aid. The 'oil-for-food' programme approved by the UN in 1996 was supposed to remedy that to a limited extent. But few people know that only part of the proceeds from Iraq's oil sales is available for humanitarian purposes because sums to compensate victims of Iraq's aggression against Kuwait and pay off UN costs are deducted first. Still, the aid is useful and has resulted in a certain improvement in supply. Whoever reports that must expect censure from those critics of the UN for whom the fact that aid is reaching that people affected does not fit their negative enemy image.

The debate on whether the sanctions against Iraq have led to a threefold or five-fold increase in child mortality can be left to the experts. Rightly, UNICEF, the WHO and others have highlighted these figures because they in particular grab public attention. But one should realise that these statistics are only and indication of the dreadful worsening of the overall health situation of the people of Iraq over the last decade. Before the Gulf war, Iraq was relatively prosperous, its public health service was well staffed and well equipped and able to offer the people comprehensive free healthcare at a good level. It is now totally ruined. Malnutrition and poor drinking water quality have led to an increase in many illnesses on a sometimes-epidemic scale. Hospitals are unable to function due to a lack of equipment and medicines.

The decline of the public health service is in turn also only an indication of the general shortcomings in Iraq that is expressed equally in a run-down school system, widespread unemployment and other social dislocation such as the gradual disappearance of small to medium-sized businesses and an increase in crime.

Reform Proposals are on the Table

Three years ago, a group of American academics presented a list of indicators aimed at helping to establish the starting point and impact of sanctions in the social sector. Among other things, it was meant to point out the vulnerabilities of endangered sections of populations and enable recommendations of the design of sanction regimes. The report offered some telling and cogent indicators for the sectors of public health, the economy, migration movements, politics and humanitarian aid. Most of these indicators were registered by UN specialist organisation. The intention now is to incorporate such information as standards in the consultation and decision processes of the Security Council.

For here it is a question of fundamental human rights which the international community must respect. The people threatened or affected by sanctions have compelling rights (jus cogens). First of all, these are the right to life, good health, food, water, housing and clothing. Starving a people must never be permitted. The limits of sanctions are clearly overstepped when a considerable section of the population drops below the subsistence level. With regard to Iraq, there has been growing criticism in recent years that the Security Council has not met fully its responsibility for the consequences of its actions. The UN's economic sanctions were at any rate from the time that they led to life-threatening impacts for the Iraqi civil population, and in particular to an empirically verifiable reduction of life expectancy due to lack of and under-supply of the people, as well as an increase in child mortality, a violation of the right to life and thus are to be judged as unlawful.

It is morally and legally untenable to treat the people of so-called 'rogue states' inhumanly or to make humanitarian aid subject to political changes, as recently in Yugoslavia. Whoever does that is himself a rogue. Sanctions must not be used, as to date, as what Boutros-Ghali called a "blunt instrument". They should above all hit decision-takers and political elites. 'Smart sanctions' are called for, and are being discussed keenly at international conferences. 'Scalpel rather than a cudgel' is the motto.

Index